King Edgar

A Life Of Regret

ALAN REED

WestBow Press books may be ordered through booksellers or by contacting:

WestBow Press
A Division of Thomas Nelson & Zondervan
1663 Liberty Drive
Bloomington, IN 47403
www.westbowpress.com
1 (866) 928-1240

ISBN: 978-1-5127-1897-3 (sc)
ISBN: 978-1-5127-1899-7 (hc)
ISBN: 978-1-5127-1898-0 (e)

Library of Congress Control Number: 2015918557

Print information available on the last page.

WestBow Press rev. date: 11/30/2015

Dedication

This book is dedicated to all the Borthwicks everywhere, and there are a good number in the United Kingdom, the United States, Canada, Australia, and, after that, all around the world.

Special dedication goes to the parents of my wife, Bonnie and Murray Borthwick, who in May and June of 2014, around their sixty-fifth wedding anniversary, traded away their small, earthbound apartment and worldly troubles for a mansion in heavenly splendor, where their health will be perfect.

Acknowledgments

After working in industry all my life, I can't even begin to try to explain the difference between speaking with people in that sector and speaking with any of my new friends at WestBow Press: Matt Temple, Barbra Carter, Rosalie White, and Tim Fitch. They were polite and kind and always made feel better after I had called upon them. With Rosalie's help, I managed to create five illustrations, even when she and I could only communicate at long distance. If only the whole world could be like this. Thank you to my friends.

My daughter Kirsten was a student in architecture at the University of Tennessee and has developed some interesting artistic talents. I found that her drawing of a tree in cold weather would be easily adapted to use as the front and back cover of this book, as the story is set during Christmastime.

Kirsten then showed my wife and I something that she has called "Photoshop on stencil," a way of making a black-and-white portrait from a color photograph. I knew I just had to find a way to include this type of work in the book. And I found that the process was some fun. The first example is the image of Queen Ingigerd receiving Edmund and Edward. I placed my daughter-in-law Leslie in the role of the Good Queen. My grandson Wes is superb as the toddler Edmund, and my grandson Murray is brilliant in the place of the infant Edward.

Then my wife, Barbara, mentioned to our friend Mary at our church that we were writing a book about Scotland. Mary was interested, as her family has a Scottish name and as several of the family have gorgeous red hair. Because of this, my imagination hit on an idea; if I could borrow one of Mary's family portraits, those people would be a perfect match for the royal family of Edward the Exile when he left Hungary in 1056. I am very grateful to Mary and her family.

When I let some of my family preview this book, they were confused by the names and relationships of the historical figures. To clarify this, I asked Kirsten to create the three family trees that you will find.

Author's Note

I did most of my research for this book by using the Internet. As with many other things, there is a good side and a bad side when using this resource.

The good side is that one can quickly access several different websites to collect information on the topic or person that one is studying. It is after this that the problems start. The various websites present information that usually agrees on the basics, but after that the stories can diverge to some extent, finally becoming contradictory from site to site. One would think that when looking at people who lived, and at history that took place, more than nine hundred years ago, the story would be known and consistent. But I often found it challenging to try to determine what a consensus of the information would consist of.

In some cases, I can see that there legitimate reasons why various theories can develop around what historians attempt to retell. Documentation of events and genealogies from the time when King Edgar lived are extremely limited. But after that, the information on the websites becomes even worse as modern writers start to project their modern agendas onto their reporting. Here is the most glaring example:

Edward the Martyr was assassinated in 978, but sometime in 2011 or 2012 he was assassinated again. In late 2009, I printed the story of Edward because I was very thrilled by the reports of his character and of the miracles that occurred. Recently checking the website on which I had first found the information, I was stunned to read that now Edward had been an extremely angry young man. The kind testimony to his character was gone, the miracles were gone, and even the fact that he had been canonized as a saint was gone. Can "revisionist history" exist?

When writing about a subject like history, the writer is expected to use footnotes or endnotes to reference the sources of information that he or she consulted when writing of the story. When I began to provide my sources in notes, I found that I was frequently providing Internet addresses. I soon found that Internet addresses change often.

I also used several books as references. The books I found provided only pieces of the story that I was looking for. Also, I considered some of the information to be questionable or contradictory. The history that I present seemed the most accurate and made the most sense to me after I evaluated all the information about King Edgar that I could find.

Preface

A very logical question to ask would be this: Why would a mostly ordinary man living in Tennessee write a book about an obscure English king who lived long ago? The answer begins with my wife, who is one of the Borthwick clan.

My wife's grandfather was William Borthwick, a man who was born in Ayr, Scotland, in 1899. He was baptized at St. Giles Cathedral, a magnificent church in the center of Edinburgh. In the early 1900s, his family, part of the huge wave of immigration from Europe to the New World around that time, left Scotland and arrived in Canada. The family moved to Midland, Michigan, after World War I. Ironically, about the same time, my mother's family, the Hendersons, left England and also arrived in Canada. My mother was born on Prince Edward Island in 1917. Shortly after that, the Hendersons moved to the United States, near Chicago, Illinois.

When William Borthwick moved to Michigan, he had the extraordinary luck and blessing to meet Jeanne, who soon became his bride. Not only was Jeanne a Scottish woman, but also she had more recently come from Scotland and had retained the very noticeable accent (or brogue) that characterizes the way English is spoken by the Scottish. In fact, as my wife's father and aunt were growing up, Jeanne's accent was so difficult to understand that the children in her family often would have to ask her to repeat what she had said.

The Scottish influence remained strong in the family even after my wife was born. Jeanne had several relatives still living in Scotland who were able to make the visit to their extended family in Michigan. That resulted in a houseful of people speaking "Scottish." And they all loved bagpipes. The sound of the bagpipes blaring (I can't stand bagpipes) will always gain their rapt attention!

So my wife always had hope that she could make her dream trip to Scotland. Around 1996, we became aware that the Borthwick Castle, located about twelve miles southeast of Edinburgh, had become a bed-and-breakfast type of lodge. At that point, the trip to Scotland moved up from being merely a "bucket list" item and took on the identity of a "pilgrimage".

By 2009 we were able to make the trip to Scotland. We toured Edinburgh, Loch Ness, and the Isle of Skye. We visited numerous castles and learned about Scotland's history. We bought souvenirs, tried the food, and spent a lot of money. And we stayed two nights at the Borthwick Castle, which became one of the highlights of the trip. While we were staying at the castle, we were able to visit the Borthwick Parish Church, which is on the road where a lengthy driveway starts toward the castle. We purchased a booklet containing a history of the church. At another location, we purchased a booklet about the history of the Borthwick clan. After arriving home, I finally was able to take time to read these and several other printed items that we had bought. I found the following items that seemed to begin to tell a story.

From the history of the parish church, I found that the first written confirmation of a church being located at this site is dated 1153. However, it is known, at least in legend, that the church was part of a donation made in 1150. Even well before that, there came an authority from King David I of Scotland that could have created the church as early as 1124. In the book about the Borthwick clan I read, it is "thought that" the Borthwick family was descended from a man named Andreas who came from Hungary with Edgar Aethling. So who was Edgar Aethling? It turns out that Edgar was the king of England for a very brief time. He spent the last years of his life in Scotland. It is thought that Edgar was in Scotland when he died in 1125 or 1126. Edgar would have been a friend of the family that became the Borthwicks. So there; I conclude that it's just barely possible that Edgar was present at the very start of the church that is now the Borthwick Parish Church.

I was educated to be an engineer, so the phrase "it is thought that" is very unsatisfactory to me. I want things to be precise, to fit together, and to work all the time. When it comes to history, I want to know what happened, what caused it to happen, and the date when it happened. I want the history written year after year, in order. I want to know the dates when people were born and when they died. If it's genealogy, I want to know who begat whom, and who were the good guys and who were the bad guys. I want it all shown for me. Thus, I started typing what I had learned so that I could organize the fragments of history and the stories I heard, thereby blending them in a written history.

Starting with the Borthwicks, all we know about Andreas the Hungarian is what I have already written. If someone were to take on the project of writing a fictional tale or making a movie about his adventures and his life, as well as about the lives of many other people discussed in this book, then the final product would be a series of interesting subjects. I, however, am not at all interested in fiction, even though this book will likely be considered fiction. Two sections of this book, "Edgar Reminisces" and "Edgar's Message," which are in the area of imagination and must certainly be considered fiction, contain ideas that King Edgar could have plausibly articulated in 1124.

However, concerning Edgar Aetheling, history does record a few things. Now Edgar's reign as King of England can be satisfactorily covered in a history book by no more than an asterisked statement and a footnote. But we do know a few more historical facts about him. Plus, after I read several more of those "it was thought that" ideas, I found just enough for me to see the incredible figure that Edgar was. I became fascinated with him and began researching the men who were kings at that time. I even began to identify with Edgar as I tried to understand his thoughts and feelings. Why, Edgar and I have learned some of the same things! I began to blend some of my own experiences with Edgar's life. So what caused me to feel like I could identify with Edgar?

I would say that I am able to find comfort in my life, as the things that have happened to me are far less troubling than the things that happened to Edgar. For example, when I was seventeen, my mother fell ill and passed away rather quickly. That is my personal tragedy, but I don't consider it to be a particularly severe event. When tragedy found Edgar, though, he was a *small boy,* and the effect on him was like an avalanche sweeping away his entire future. As another example:

I have had a fine career in engineering, but at times I have had my feelings of disappointment and frustration. I have even had *feelings* of failure. But when I failed, the problem was corrected by an addition to the contract and the expenditure of some money. In Edgar's adult life, his failures *cost many men their lives.* And conflict came often to Edgar. Until he reached his late forties, he experienced nothing but loss. Disappointment slapped Edgar's face from side to side; failure kicked Edgar in the gut over and over.

One could make the joke that Edgar's life was a shipwreck, but in fact he *was in two shipwrecks at sea* and nearly lost his life on each occasion.

The things that happened to Edgar were not his fault, but for a long time in his life disaster seemed to follow him. "If it weren't for bad luck, he would have had no luck at all" is an old American joke, one that seems to apply to Edgar.

Leo Durocher, the manager of the perennially losing Chicago Cubs baseball team, was trying to rally his players to greater effort when he bellowed, "Nice guys finish last," a quotation for which he will always be remembered. Edgar *was* this nice guy.

I have come to realize that one learns life's lessons more from trials and failures than one learns from life's successes. Thus, considering the things that Edgar experienced, I believe that he can teach us a lot, even if he was influenced by the times of the 1050s through the 1120s.

There is another way that I found myself identifying with Edgar: I am a Christian. I am convinced that Edgar had a strong Christian faith, as his family and the king that he knew as a child were known to be fully devoted to the faith. In fact, the king Edward the Confessor that Edgar knew as a child and his sister Margaret were both *canonized as saints in the Roman Catholic Church.* This fact had to have made a huge spiritual impact on Edgar. As a result of my affinity with Edgar, this book is written from a believer's viewpoint. In it, I present what I believe Edgar would have had to say about his faith.

I could find no history book or Internet source that presented the complete history of the aforementioned time period in a way that satisfactorily covered the events and figures I found interesting. Eventually, I determined to write what I knew about the history and also to include my imagination of Edgar's memoirs. I just wrote what I wanted to write. Thus, my book is very unusual to classify, as it contains elements of both nonfiction and fiction.

This book is divided into four sections. In the first section, "The History," I present a combination of history and Edgar's biography—a "histo-biography," if you will. There are astonishing stories of the English kings and their frequent struggles to get into the line of succession and to ascend to the throne. Sometimes I found the facts of the actual history to be almost unbelievable, inspirational, and even miraculous. As is the case with the Bible, the history of King Edgar forces one to believe the story, including the miracles, as I find it hard to believe that someone could make up those stories and as the miracles were witnessed by a number of people. This was a time when the Christian faith was credited with being a huge and even deciding factor working throughout all of this history. Also in this section I frequently provide quotations from historical narratives of the time, as these add color and feeling, given the language of the period. I do show some of the interpersonal relationships that seem to be glossed over in the recorded history. I also offer enough comments to keep the story on track, allowing it to proceed in an historically accurate straight line.

I can even claim some possibly new scholarship; I have listed by name several men who traveled with Edward the Exile from Hungary to England, and provided an idea for how the name King Arthur was created. These are very tiny pieces of history which I have not found previously covered. Of course, these may have been written somewhere that I have not been able to access.

The second and third parts of the book are set in the year 1124. The church that will become the Borthwick Parish Church is celebrating its first Christmas. I have provided Edgar with some friends and families that have fictitious names so that we can hear their interaction with Edgar. I think it is possible that Edgar helped start the church, even if just by giving a monetary gift or by providing the building as temporary shelter.

In the part of this book titled "Edgar Reminisces," Edgar recalls many of his past experiences and tries to impress the lessons he learned from these upon John, the priest in training, and the children who are present. The adults who are present include two of Edgar's former knights and an elderly woman who was Andreas's younger sister and was one of the group that came from Hungary. The discussion touches almost every imaginable subject from church to war.

In the part titled "Edgar's Message," we see Edgar trying to inspire people and give them hope for the new church. His viewpoint is completely unique. Some of his ideas might even be considered modern, although other ideas and things that he talks about are very medieval. His message includes participation from those listening to him, so this section of the book reads more like a conversation than as a speech.

Sometimes I have thought that "Edgar Reminisces" and "Edgar's Message" together could be presented as a play that would not be too difficult to produce, as it would require a rather simple set. A group of people with some interest in acting and some energy to develop the characters could accomplish the presentation. The most important character is Edgar, of course, so the play would need just one very capable actor to play the lead role and several other actors to play the supporting roles.

This book's epilogue, "The Families," is a very brief look at five families who traveled from Europe to England and then went on to Scotland during Edgar's time. These are some interesting stories that I came across while researching the material for this book. They seem to be best described by looking back from the current time into history, rather than making an attempt to integrate them into the history.

There are some amazing stories throughout the book, so let's begin!

England and Scotland

The History

To provide a running start to this story, a look at some English history is required. This will help if you are like me. When looking at English history, I could recognize only the year 1066, the Battle of Hastings, and William the Conqueror—and not much of anything else. I will attempt to keep this section lively with my writing style.

Cerdic & The House of Wessex

In the beginning (it seems that all books should start this way), i.e., in the time of the 480s AD, a man named Cerdic living on the English island became king over a small area that was probably not much larger than the area his family had held and that was similar in size to other small kingdoms existing at that time. It is known that Cerdic traveled to France. He apparently received some authority from the Roman emperor, as he received the title of *ealdormen* (our word *alderman* derives from this word), a relatively junior rank. He recruited some soldiers and, because of this, several ships were required when he returned to southern England in the year AD 495. Cerdic had a personality and connections that allowed him to forge some alliances with several different family groups. When necessary, Cerdic and his men were able to win some battles over small bands of resistance. By the year AD 519, Cerdic could claim that he was the first king of England. His reign established the first unified and independent kingdom to govern a large area on the sparsely populated island of England.

The English kingdom grew from the area south and west of London called Wessex, and thus Cerdic and his descendants became the line of royals known as the "House of Wessex." Kings belonging to the House of Wessex would rule England, with some interruptions, until 1066.

There are several striking parallels between the life of Cerdic and the life of the legendary figure King Arthur, so much so that I believe Cerdic is almost certainly the same person as the legendary Arthur. These similarities include the exact same time period of their conquests, 500 to AD 530; many of the same (or close) locations of their battles and oft-visited places; and similar names of their family and friends. Perhaps the title of *ealdormen* was changed to "Arthurman" and then to "King Arthurman." If one is a king, one's title doesn't also have to include the word *man*, so Cerdic could have become known as "King Arthur." The article "Cerdic, King of the West Saxons" makes a lengthy comparison of Cerdic and King Arthur.[1]

Edward the Martyr

My look at a portion of the continuous history shall begin with Edward the Martyr, who was born around AD 962. In starting with this date, I am beginning the story earlier than I need to, but the story surrounding Edward is so astonishing, marked with miracles and healing, that it deserves to be retold. And it is possible to view the brief life of Edward as a possible beginning of the end of the House of Wessex.

Edward's father was King Edgar the Peaceable (not the Edgar who is featured in our story), and his mother was Queen Ethelflaed,[2] who died not long after Edward's birth in 963 or 964. After about two years, Edgar married a woman named Elfthryth.[3] Edgar and Elfthryth had a son named Aethelred, who was about five years younger than Edward. In 975, King Edgar, still only in his early 30's, died. At the age of about thirteen, the Witenagemot, or "wise men," the ruling council of England, met and ratified the selection of Edward as the new king of England.

Edgar the Peaceful's Family Tree

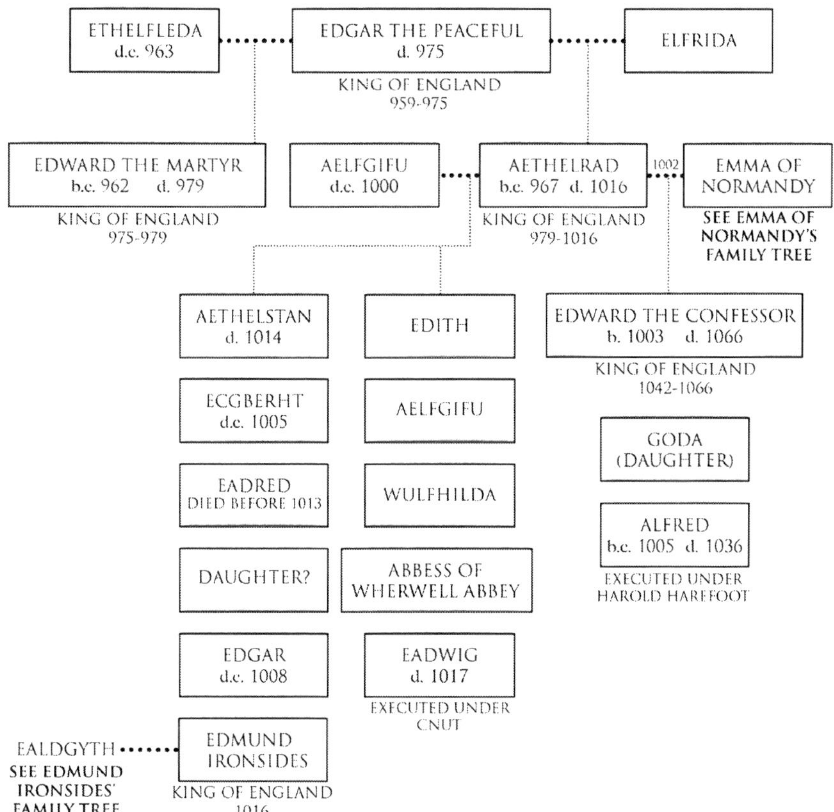

created by kirsten reed

Now Edward was most decidedly not the average teenager. Instead, he was an exceptional young man, especially in his devotion to the Christian faith. He lived during a time and in a geographical area when there was considerable pressure on everyone to be a Christian. In addition, the deaths that occurred frequently to people of all ages in an era nearly devoid of medical care provided a constant reminder of life and death and the need to commune often with God. Edward's father, Edgar the Peaceable, had been a devout believer, and his influence continued to guide Edward. Here is a testimonial about Edward's character and piety written by one of his contemporaries.

> St. Edward was a young man of great devotion and excellent conduct; he was wholly Catholic, good and of holy life; moreover, above all things he loved God and the Church; he was generous to the poor, a haven to the good, a champion of the Faith of Christ, a vessel full of every virtuous grace. He was an earnest supporter of the monastics in the life of the Church, as his father had been before him.[4]

However, there had previously been disagreement between those who supported Edward's claim to the throne and those who thought that his half-brother Aethelred should be king. The archbishop of Canterbury at the time, St. Dunstan, was a prominent supporter of Edward. Those supporting Aethelred were considered to be the "irreligious" in England.

The dispute about who should become king developed into a conflict that was started by Elfhere, a prominent nobleman. Edward's father, King Edgar, had provided land to establish monasteries, but Elfhere and his men destroyed those monasteries to reclaim the land. The monks living in the monasteries were quickly evicted. Edward became very angry about this conflict. Given that his deceased father's religious work was being trashed immediately after the his passing, Edward's anger can certainly be understood. Edward probably knew many of the monks who were now having to find new homes.

Edward's stepmother, Elfthryth, found another reason to be opposed to her stepson. Desiring that she should be royal and have a royal lifestyle for herself, she became determined that her son Aethelred should be king. As the two young men were not far apart in age, she began to consider what sort of action would be necessary to make this happen.

In the midmorning hours of March 18, 978, Elfthryth found an opportunity to carry out her evil intentions. Edward, enjoying recreation by riding a horse, happened to ride close to Corfe Castle, where Elfthryth lived. Seeing Edward, Elfthryth called out to him to come get a cup of mead. (Mead is a fermented drink made with honey and water—a very tasty treat.) Unsuspecting, Edward rode over to Elfthryth. As he was accepting the cup of mead, Elfthryth—or, more likely, an accomplice—was able to come close enough alongside the horse to thrust a dagger into the middle of Edward's chest. Edward tried to ride away, but he quickly slumped to the side of the horse. The startled horse bolted and began galloping. It then dragged Edward, who had his foot tangled in the stirrup, along the ground. The horse stampeded wildly, finally stopping once it reached the middle of a stream. Now Elfthryth had only one more problem: what to do with Edward's body.

"My name is Anne. I am a very simple lady whose purpose is to pray. What you need to know about me is this: I have been blind my entire life. I lived in a small house where I could easily feel my way along when I moved. Other people had taken me to their homes and castles. I could feel that those places were much larger than my house. These people told me that with their sense of sight, they could feel something without touching it at all. They can see trees and animals without touch, and they see the warmth of the sun.

One night, everything changed for me! Elfthryth and some men came to my house during the day. She wanted to visit me and see how I was feeling. The group left in a hurry to go somewhere else. That very night, a brightness filled my house. It was as if I could see it, but I was very afraid. I called out, "Lord have mercy. Lord have mercy on me!" Suddenly I could see! My hand reached for the table, and the table was exactly where I saw it. I could touch the wall, and it was where I saw it. Then I saw that something was under my table. Soon I could determine that this was a person such as I am! Who was this? The person was dead. What a horror! I stayed awake and watched the sun rise. How glorious it is to see the sun, the castles, the trees! As soon as I could find Elfthryth at her castle, I told her that I had received my healing! Of course I asked who the person under my table was. Her reaction seemed angry to me. She gathered three men in front of her. While I continued to try to show my joy, she was "troubled and again ordered the disposal of the body."[5] Elfthryth assured me that she would clean my house. She ordered me to stay in her castle until she returned. Then she left with the men. Some time passed. When the group returned, they had all of my belongings with them. Elfthryth gave me a room in her castle. She ordered me not to mention to anyone anything about the man who had been placed in my house. But I soon

found out that this man had been Edward the king. Eventually I was able to tell everyone about the healing of my eyesight and what had appeared to happen to our beloved king."

Edward's body was moved to a wilderness area that has been described as either swampy or forested and hidden. Elfthryth and her accomplices tried to keep the secret of his murder from the rest of the English population. Eventually, the church of St. Edward at Corfe was built on the site of the little house where Anne had lived. Today, that same church stands.

Edward was nearly forgotten. But then another miracle happened. Almost two years had passed since his murder (there is a question here, as it is possible to find both 978 and 979 given as the year of Edward's assassination) when the following happened:

> A pillar of fire was seen over the place where the body was hidden, lighting up the whole area. This was seen by some of the inhabitants of Wareham, who raised the body. Immediately a clear spring of healing water sprang up in that place. Accompanied by what was now a huge crowd of mourners, the body was taken to the church of the Most Holy Mother of God in Wareham and buried at the east end of the church. This took place on February 13, 980.[6]

This miracle is said to have occurred at night in February, when the sky darkens early. People in those times had no sources of light other than torches, but in the midst of a pitch-black wilderness, the people of Wareham were able to find Edward's body.

The devout inhabitants who found Edward's body had been his religious supporters. Soon they were able to figure out the story of his murder. Elfthryth's culpability became known, and the news of this spread throughout England. The idea was advanced to remember Edward as "the Martyr," for people believed that Elfthryth murdered him on account of his Christian faith.

People who visited the place in the stream where Edward's horse had stopped found that the water provided miracles of healing.

Elfhere, the nobleman who had previously opposed Edward, was repentant about having started the conflict about who, Edward or

Aethelred, should become king. He helped to determine that Edward's body should be moved to a larger church, one at Shaftesbury.

In February 981, almost three years after Edward's death, Edward's body was found to be "completely incorrupt," which caused great joy among those who sought to relocate it. Once his body was lifted onto a bier, the procession began (on February 13, 981). The people arrived at Shaftesbury seven days later, on February 20. Then this happened: "On the way from Wareham to Shaftesbury, a further miracle had also taken place; "two crippled men were brought close to the bier and those carrying it lowered the body to their level, where upon the cripples were immediately restored to full health."[7]

Edward's body was placed beneath a tombstone near the altar of the church of a monastery. As Edward's fame increased, many pilgrims, even from other places across Europe, came to Shaftesbury to worship at the site. Also, miracles continued to occur. The monastery was rededicated to the Mother of God and to Edward.

Aethelred's mother, Elfthryth, tried visit Shaftesbury to ask forgiveness and show repentance, but she found that she was stopped by a supernatural force at a place where she could not continue, whether on horseback or on foot. Then in sincere repentance, she founded two convents. She gave up the royal life as Queen Mother and then lived the remainder of her life as a nun at one of her convents.

Even yet more astounding, it is said that in 1001 the tombstone above Edward's body in the church would rise and light would show from around the perimeter. It was as if the stone began to levitate, except that people in 1001 had no word to express levitation. Even King Aethelred heard about the miracle, and was thrilled. The king and other witnesses felt that Edward was expressing his desire to be raised. On June 20 of that year, the tomb was opened. Those present stated that such a fragrance arose that they felt a sensation of being in paradise. The relics of Edward's body were then placed in a coffin. There was another procession before his re-internment.

In 1008, an all-England council of the Catholic Church officially glorified Edward as a saint. Within the church, a span of about 30 years after someone has passed is lightning speed for such recognition to be granted. Thus, Saint Edward the Martyr is recognized by both the Roman Catholic and the Eastern Orthodox Churches, since he was canonized before the church split during the Great Schism[8] that occurred in 1054. Today, Edward's memory and relics are kept by the Saint Edward Brotherhood (a Russian Orthodox community) in Brookwood, England.

Should we believe that the miracles described above actually happened? The miracles that have been described are striking enough to be considered of a biblical scale. But all the occasions that I have described were witnessed by numbers of people, not just by individuals. This fact places these miracles on a level with the miracles of the Bible.

The Anglo-Saxon Chronicle was a document maintained(intended to be annually) as a history of the English people. Oftentimes, the writers would add their own commentaries. The writer of the entry below offered the following amazing commentary with a religious perspective:

> No worse deed than this [the murder of Edward] was ever done by the English nation, since they first sought the land of Britain. Men murdered him, but God has magnified him. He was in life an earthly king—he is now after death a heavenly saint. Him would not his earthly relatives avenge—but his Heavenly Father has avenged him amply. The earthly homicides would wipe out his memory upon earth; but the avenger above has spread his memory abroad, in the heavens and in the earth. Those, Who would not now before bow to his living body, now bow on their the knee to his dead bones. Now can we perceive that the wisdom of men, their meditations, and their counsels, are as naught against the appointment of God.[9]

The archbishop of Canterbury, Dunstan, who had supported Edward's claim to the throne, was greatly saddened by Edward's sudden disappearance and spoke of his "great sorrow" at Aethelred's coronation. Later, a chronicler would credit Dunstan with these startling words:

> Because thou(Aethelred) hast been raised to the throne by the death of your brother, whom thy mother has slain, therefore now hear the word of the Lord; thus saith the Lord: the sword shall not depart from thy house, but shall

> rage against thee all the days of thy life, cutting off thy seed, until thy kingdom become the kingdom of an alien, whose customs and tongue the nation which thou rulest knoweth not. And thy sin, and the sin of thy mother, and the sin of the men who were parties to her wickedness, shall be expiated only by long continued punishment.[10]

This statement sounds like it came straight out of the Bible. This was crafted by a writer who likely took pride in his creation of a biblical prophecy applied to England. He placed this quotation in his chronicle *after* Aethelred had died(1016); thus, the presentation was from the viewpoint of looking back and knowing the "fulfillment" of the prophecy. This statement also shows how prevalent Christianity was in the minds of the people, even the scholars. The religious people completely accepted the idea that God rewarded faithfulness and severely punished sin by way of the events that followed.

Unable to adjust to the magnitude of the crime of Edward's murder, the justice system in England broke down. Apparently, no one thought to charge or arrest anyone for Edward's assassination. The perpetrators got away with murder even after people realized who the guilty parties were.

Image of Edward the Martyr.
Kindly provided courtesy of the St. Edward Brotherhood in Brookwood, England.

Aethelred the Unready

Aethelred was thirteen or fourteen years old when he became king of England. Far from pleased to become king, he was so grieved by the loss of his half-brother that it is said, "He could not stop weeping. This angered his mother, who took some candles and beat him with them viciously, hoping thereby to stem the flow of his tears. It is said that thereafter Ethelred so hated candles that he would never allow them to be lit in his presence."[11]

Aethelred's epithet "the Unready" actually did not exist until it was penned by thirteenth-century historians many years after Aethelred was gone. His epithet did not have anything to do with his young age when he became king. It is actually a pun on the meaning of Aethelred's name. His name means "noble counsel," and "un-red," means "no counsel" or "ill-advised counsel." Aethelred himself admitted that his advisers could and did take advantage of his ignorance, thus giving the historian the thought to create a joke.[12]

Aethelred needed no advice when it came to starting a family. He married a woman named Aelfgifu of York. The couple had six sons and five daughters. Their son Edmund would succeed Aethelred as king.

But Aelfgifu passed so in 1002 Aethelred married Emma,[13] the sister of the Duke of Normandy. Emma and Aethelred would have three children, including a son named Edward who would later become king of England. Aethelred, of course, couldn't imagine that more than sixty years in the future his connection to Normandy would radically change the course of English history.

St. Dunstan's fear of "great sorrow" after the death of Edward in 979 began to become a thought that could be considered the fulfillment of a prophecy when, after a lengthy(about 30 years) period of relative peace, the Vikings returned to raid England in 980. At first, these attacks were local, but by 991, a much larger Viking force arrived, expanding the area of the attacks. Following a large battle, Aethelred provided a monetary tribute to the Vikings as "protection money." Shown as a chart are the relevant years and the tribute monies paid in those years:

Year	Tribute Paid (in pounds)
991	10,000
994	16,000
1002	24,000
1006	36,000
1012	48,000

Given the value of money today, these numbers are not very high; however, a millennium ago these amounts were about all the money that the English treasury could muster up and pay out. Plainly, as the Viking attacks continued to increase in size, the Viking warriors' demands increased. Aethelred finally realized what another English leader in the 1930s would also discover: that appeasing one's enemy doesn't work. In 1008, he ordered a fleet of ships to be built for the defense of England, but in 1009, the Vikings landed an even larger force before the English fleet could be effective. By 1012, the Vikings controlled much of southern England. Even after receiving the enormous tribute in 1012, they still wanted more. They wanted everything.

In my imagination, I can see two young teenage girls and some small boys in the middle of a ship that is surrounded by rowing Viking sailors.

"My name is Aileen, and my sister is Mary. I have been crying so much that I cannot cry any more, but Mary is still weeping. We know that my father was killed. My mother, I believe, escaped, God help her. These men are on both sides of us and they stare at us. I cannot understand what these men are saying. I am just fourteen years old. I want to live, but now death might be better. England, my home, is now no longer in sight. Will I ever see my home again? O Lord, I have never prayed with this much determination before. Have mercy. Have your mercy on us! Amen."

Near the end of 1013, the Viking leader Swein Forkbeard[14] forced the English people to recognize him as their king. Aethelred and Emma had to flee to Normandy for safety. But in February 1014, just forty-one days after he assumed power, Forkbeard fell from his horse and died. The Witenagemot would meet and invited Aethelred to return as king, but with the admonition that he should be a better king!

But the Vikings would soon be back. This time their leader was Cnut[15] (sometimes presented as Cnute or Canute), who was the son of Swein. Aethelred did his best to defend his homeland, but the Viking leader was now able to control a large area of England. The situation for the English was even more dire in the late summer of 1015, when Aethelred's son Edmund[16] married a woman named Ealdgyth,[17] who came from a family that was opposed to Aethelred. This angered Aethelred and also had the effect of a revolt, dividing English support between Aethelred and Edmund.

Aethelred was about fifty-three years old when he died on April 23, 1016, apparently of natural causes. His son Edmund is considered to have succeeded him.

Edmund Ironsides' Family Tree

MACBETH
d. 1057
KING OF SCOTLAND
1040-1057

LULACH
d. 1058
KING OF SCOTLAND
1057-1058

EDMUND IRONSIDE
d. 1016
KING OF ENGLAND
1016

EALDGYTH
FROM EDGAR THE PEACEFUL'S FAMILY TREE

EDMUND
b. 1015 d. IN HUNGARY?

EDWARD AETHLING THE EXILE
b. 1016 d.c. 1056-57

AGATHA

DONALD III BANE
b.c. 1033 d. 1100
KING OF SCOTLAND
JOINT RULE WITH EDMUND
1093-1097

INGEBJORG
d. 1069

MALCOLM III CANMORE
b. 1031 d. 1093
KING OF SCOTLAND
1058-1093

MARGARET
b.c. 1045 d. 1093

CHRISTINA
b.c. 1048 d.c. 1100

EDGAR AETHLING
b.c. 1051 d.c. 1026
NAMED KING OF ENGLAND
1066

DUNCAN II
b. 1060 d. 1094
KING OF SCOTLAND
1094

MALCOLM

DONALD

DAUGHTER

EDMUND
b.c. 1072 d. 1100
KING OF SCOTLAND
JOINT RULE WITH DONALD III
1093-1097

EDGAR
b.c. 1075 d. 1107
KING OF SCOTLAND
1197 - 1107

ETHELRED
b.c. 1074

EDWARD
b.c. 1071 d. 1093

ALEXANDER
b.c. 1078 d. 1124
KING OF SCOTLAND
1107 - 1124

DAVID
b.c. 1083 d. 1153
KING OF SCOTLAND
1124 - 1153

MARY
b.c. 1082 d. 1116

EDITH
b.c. 1080

HENRY I
SEE EMMA OF NORMANDY'S FAMILY TREE

created by kirsten reed

Edmund Ironsides

Edmund was Aethelred's third son. Edmund was not expected to become king, but the two oldest sons had already passed before Aethelred's death. Edmund was proclaimed King of England by the people of London, as he led the defense of the city. At the same time, the Witan met at Southampton. Heavily influenced by the Vikings, they actually named Cnut as king.

During the summer of 1016, there were a series of battles in England. Unlike his father, Edmund was a shrewd leader and understood the military strategy of that era. Edmund's forces defeated the Vikings in one battle at Oxford. Several other of his battles ended as stand-offs. Thanks to Edmund's victories, the English people gave him the nickname "Ironsides," also noted as "Old Ironsides," the latter in spite of the fact that he was aged only about twenty-five. However, on October 18, Cnut's forces finally got the best of Edmund in a battle at Ashingdon (also Assandun).[18] Cnut was able to dictate terms of the subsequent peace agreement. Edmund would have the area of Wessex, and Cnut would control the rest of England. It was also agreed that in the event that one of them should die, the survivor would take control of the whole realm.

About six weeks later, on November 30, Cnut was able to have Edmund assassinated. In view of the above arrangement, Edward's having staked his kingdom and his life on a handshake with his archrival and much more powerful enemy, this does not seem to be a surprising result. Thus, Cnut the Viking was now the king of all England.

Even though Edmund and Ealdgyth had been married for only about fifteen months, they already had two sons, Edmund and Edward.[19] What would happen to them under Cnut's rule?

Cnut the Great

The Viking king Cnut was born sometime between 990 and 995 in Denmark. Surprisingly, he was actually a third-generation Christian. Living in England, Cnut found much to like about his new possession. Therefore, when the fighting ended, he began to restore peace and prosperity. Rather than suffer as a conquered nation, England became a prominent part of the Vikings' empire. Free trade between Sweden, Denmark, and England helped spur economic growth. There continued to be minor conflicts between entities seeking to control the other lands that the Vikings touched. At the height of his empire, Cnut controlled all of Denmark and Norway; all of Sweden that mattered; the Orkney Islands and the Hebrides Islands; and all of Ireland that mattered. The far northern areas of Sweden and Norway were almost unoccupied and didn't matter. Cnut made peace with the kings of Scotland, which, being sparsely populated, was not a threat.

Cnut quickly began to eliminate the surviving members of the House of Wessex. He had executed several English noblemen, including one of Aethelred's sons. He decided to send Edmund's two young sons, Edmund and Edward, back to Sweden. He wrote a note with orders stipulating what should become of them.

Cnut was married to Aelfgifu of Northhampton,[20] and they had two sons, Harold Harefoot (nicknamed "Harefoot" because of his running speed and skill at hunting),[21] who was born about 1015, and Svein Knutson, born about 1016. But when Cnut became king, another opportunity came along. In July of 1017, he married Emma of Normandy, the widow of Aethelred! The son of Cnut and Emma was Harthacnut,[22] who was born in June of 1018. Cnut designated Harthacnut to be his successor over Aelfgifu's sons. But even though Cnut was their stepfather, Emma's sons Edmund and Alfred were forced into exile in Normandy among Emma's relatives.

Cnut ruled over the Viking Empire until he died on November 12, 1035, at Shaftesbury.

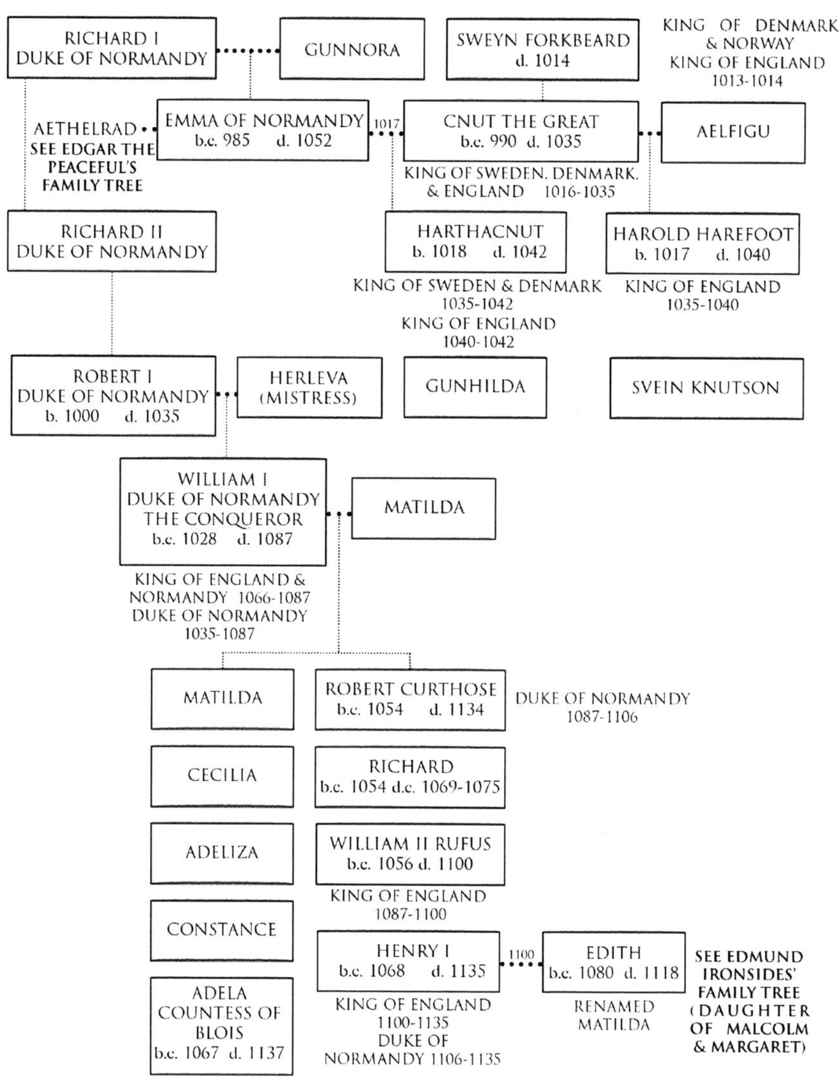

Queen Ingigerd

Viking ships carrying Edmund and Edward landed in Sweden near the home of young Queen Ingigerd.[23] To illustrate the scene, let's suppose that Edmund is about twenty-four months and Edward is about four months of age when they arrive in Sweden.

The queen is in her home with several of her maids and servants when news comes that ships from England have arrived. The arrival of ships is an event in itself, so the queen sends several of her servants to the docks to see who has arrived and what they have brought. Presently, the servants return. One is carrying an infant wrapped in blankets. Two other servants have a very small boy walking between them, hand in hand. The queen's protective and maternal instincts immediately kick in.

"Come to me, young man. Servants, let me hold the infant. I would like to have a family someday and now I have two sons come to me without cost."

She asks the young man his name. The child is extremely shy and says nothing. With some coaxing and help from a translator, the boy finally responds. The baby is uncomfortable and crying, so the queen uses her best baby talk until she makes the little one smile. At this moment, when the queen is just beginning to establish some communication with the two boys, a courier comes and announces that he has a letter from Cnut regarding the boys. Queen Ingigerd reads the letter.

> *To My Subjects in Sweden:*
>
> *The older boy is Edmund, and the infant is Edward. They are the sons of the English King Edmund, whom we killed. Execute them immediately! And keep this quiet, since I don't want to upset the English people.*
>
> *Cnut*

I can just imagine the Queen's response:

"What? Execute these little darlings? Cnut, what are you thinking about? We are Christians and Vikings, not savages! I'm taking care of these boys! And I'm engaged to a king in Norway, but now we Swedes have a border dispute with the Norwegians. I have got to get out of that too. I'm leaving! Norway is to the west, England is to the west; I'm going east. I am so out of here."

By 1019, the queen and the boys had traveled to Kiev, Russia! Now that would be a safe distance from Cnut in England!

Most surely, when Cnut gave an order he expected it to be carried out without fail and without question. But to Queen Ingigerd, this case was going to be an exception. She believed that these boys were too cute to harm and that some way had to be found to save them. Ingigerd herself was only about sixteen or seventeen years old, so she was not experienced at using violence and warfare as a solution to problems.

Queen Ingigerd was charmed; she was not going to allow the toddler Edmund and the infant Edward to be executed.
Used by kind permission of Leslie Reed. created by kirsten reed

The queen married Grand Prince Yaroslav, also known as Yaroslav I or Yaroslav the Wise, in Kiev.[24] The queen and Yaroslav had six sons and five daughters. Three of their daughters became queens in the countries of Norway, Hungary, and France. Ingigerd may have been the mother of Agatha, who married the younger brother, Edward. Ingigerd also founded churches in Kiev and Novgorod, Russia. Much later, the queen was canonized as a saint and was given the name St. Anna.

Apparently, other members of Ingigerd's family or her friends took the boys to Hungary. Even when the brothers were in Hungary, Queen

Ingigerd remained in close contact with them. Hungary was a safe choice, as the country was ruled by King Stephen I,[25] who was making a concerted effort to advance the cause of Christianity and the church. Once there, Edmund and Edward started growing as members of a royal family. But through all of their travels, the boys' identities were maintained, even when they easily could have become anonymous. Why would the Hungarians continue to identify the boys as English royalty? The relationships between royal family lines was important to generating goodwill between, and making allies with, other nations. Peace can be better maintained among different countries when the royals of each country have royal relatives in the other countries. In this case, however, England and Hungary are such a long distance from each other that an alliance would scarcely seem to matter. No matter; the boys were safe and began to grow up in Hungary.

Harold and Harthacnut

When Cnut died in 1035, he was between forty and forty-five years old. His chosen son Harthacnut, at about the age of eighteen, became king of the Viking Empire. But there were problems in trying to control the far-flung Viking Empire. Harthacnut was in Denmark leading the resistance to a war against Norway and Sweden, so Harold Harefoot became the effective king of England simply by being there when Cnut died. He even forced Harthacnut's mother, Emma, back into exile in Normandy. But Harold died on March 17, 1040, at the age of about twenty-three.

Harthacnut, now the king of England, returned to London. Fortunately, peace had been restored in Denmark. Once again, the Viking Empire was effectively reunited. Harthacnut brought his mother, Emma, and his half-brother Edmund back from exile. He made a treaty with Edward decreeing that the English throne was to go to Edward if Harthacnut died with no legitimate male heir. But only a bit more than two years after Harold had passed, on June 8, 1042, Harthacnut died at the age of almost exactly twenty-four, and Edward was made king.[26] The House of Wessex once again ascended the throne of England!

Maybe Edward could bring some stability, as the position of King of England was proving to be very adversely affecting the life expectancy of the men in power.

Edward the Confessor

Edward, the oldest son of Aethelred and Emma, was born in about 1004. As we have already seen, he was forced into exile in Normandy by the end of 1016. He was about twelve years old when this happened. Emma had a number of relatives living in Normandy, so it would have been easy to find accommodation for Edmund and his brother Alfred. Edmund had to stay in Normandy until 1040, so he became deeply influenced by the culture and made numerous friends there.

The Viking Empire contracted after the death of Harthacnut. There would be more Viking kings who would claim the English crown, but there was no effective Viking threat to England again until 1066. Edward and the English people would enjoy freedom in their own nation.

Edward's nickname "the Confessor" developed as people saw his devotion to the Christian faith.

In 1045, Edward married Edith,[27] the daughter of nobleman Earl Godwin.[28] Soon thereafter, Earl Godwin's second son, Harold, became Edward's main adviser. Harold's last name became Godwinson, as he was "the son of Godwin."[29]

Several years after their wedding, Edward and Edith remained unable to conceive any children. One of the requirements of the king and queen is to produce sons in order to continue the royal lineage. The threat that the throne could again become vacant and be left without a successor was a serious concern. Any such a vacancy could provoke a war. Since Edward had connections to Normandy, in 1051 he gave his promise to William, Duke of Normandy[30] that he would succeed him to the throne of England.

Seal of Edward the Confessor. Our most "authentic" image of him.
Used by kind permission of Yeoman Bill Norton.
(yeomenoftheguard.com/edward12.jpg)

Edward the Exile

Meanwhile, back in Hungary, at least one of the two boys was growing up. The older boy, Edmund, simply vanished into the mist of history. However, the younger boy, Edward, was growing and prospering.

Stephen I ruled Hungary from 1000 to 1038. He significantly expanded Christian influence and the church throughout the country, and he was eventually canonized as a saint in the Catholic Church. Stephen I was followed by Peter Orseolo,[31] who continued to support and extend Christianity. Thus, Edward enjoyed the mercy of the Hungarians. He would have been trained in all the principal beliefs of the Christian faith.

Sometime between 1040 and 1044, Edward married a lady named Agatha. Historians have many theories as to where Agatha came from, but one thing seems certain: she had been born and raised in a royal family that had lived somewhere in central or eastern Europe.[32] One thought is that she was the daughter of Queen Ingigerd. That Edward was able to marry into the nobility is further proof that his identity as English royalty had been carefully maintained. Edward and Agatha adopted the name Aethling, which means "royal blood." It would certainly be a fitting name for a couple who were trying to hold onto their prominent position among European royalty.

Our royal family had three children, Margaret,[33] born about 1044; Christina,[34] born about 1047; and Edgar,[35] the subject of this book, born sometime in 1050 or 1051. So, after this lengthy story, we have finally found the answer to our first question, of how a king of England was born in Hungry. Now I ask, how does Edgar get back to England?

Hungary

Castle Reka is near the small town of Mecsekna'dasd. This is considered the birthplace of Margaret, Christina and Edgar.

Our royal family lived in some prosperity at Castle Reka[36] in Hungary. Edward was nearly the same age as Andreas, who was the son-in-law of Queen Ingigerd and who married the queen's daughter Anastasia.[37] Edward is given credit for having helped Andreas rise to become the king of Hungary as Andrew I[38] in 1046. This shows the depth of a lifelong devotion between the families, from Queen Ingigerd to Edward.

As king, Andrew followed his predecessors, dedicating his life to advancing Christianity and the Catholic Church. The strict teaching of the church likely influenced Margaret and Christina, as their childhood ambition was to become nuns. This royal family, faithful Christians, awaited an opportunity to find a better position in the world of royalty.

While Edward and his family probably could have lived happily ever after easily enough by staying in Hungary, an exciting opportunity did arise for them. In about 1056, probably first by word of mouth from people who had traveled through Europe, Edward the Confessor heard that Edward was living in Hungry. This likely would have been a real surprise to him and to the English people. I doubt if very many people in England ever thought that they would once again hear from one of the two infants who had disappeared at the end of 1016. That was forty years ago. Most people in England probably had forgotten about the existence of the two boys.

The timing could not have been better. Edward the Confessor's wife Edith was only about thirty years of age at this time, but the royal couple remained childless. Edward the Exile and his family would become the family successor that was needed. Edward the Confessor gave the order: Bring them to England!

Edward the Exile and his family would need some help to get to England. According to legend, one of the men to personally deliver the communications to Hungary would be William "the Seemly" St. Clair. William was given the nickname "the Seemly" because of his "demeanor and appearance, … well-proportioned in all his members, of midle stature, faire of face, yellow hair'd."[39] He would not have undertaken the task alone, as he apparently traveled with his brothers and possibly others. St. Clair lived in Normandy. As he was a cousin of William, Duke of Normandy, he would have also been known to Edward the Confessor. But the St. Clair family actually had fought against William the Duke in a dispute over territory. William the Seemly's father had died in the fighting. The St. Clairs may have seen the safe delivery of Edward the Exile and his family as a way to stop William the Duke's ambition to expand his rule by taking England.

As travel in that era was extremely difficult, it would have taken weeks just for William St. Clair to cross Europe to reach Hungary and find our royal family.

I can scarcely imagine the excitement that our royal family experienced when St. Clair found them and then gave them an invitation to come to London. I envision a picture such as follows. The young Edgar is in the garden next to the family's castle. As everyone has to work, his job is pulling weeds, but it is very hard for him at age 5 to stay on task. He is sitting on the ground, playing with some insects. He notices that several men on horses ride up the castle. A short time later, his mother and two older sisters come running breathlessly out to the garden:

"Edgar, we're going to move to England!" his mother exclaims. ***"Edgar, Father is going to sit next to the king of England!"*** Margaret adds. It is Christina who is the most excited: ***"Then, someday, Father will be king of England!"*** And finally: ***"Edgar, someday you too will be the king of England!"***

The family was going to prepare to move from Hungary in order to find their fortune in England. If travel was difficult in 1056, then moving an entire royal family and their entourage across Europe would have been a daunting task. William St. Clair helped Edward the Exile to form an entire group to assist with the trip. This was a group of people who were dedicated to our royal family. In that age of feudalism, it is possible that everyone in the group was required to kneel and take an oath of loyalty to Edward. All of the group would also expect to remain in England as associates of Edward, seeing the idea of a return to Hungary as impossible. The commitment of every adult member of this group would be an absolute requirement. Recruiting a committed group of people such as this, and preparing to move, likely took months.

Andreas the Hungarian[40], our possible ancestor of the Borthwicks, was one of the several knights whose job it was to protect the group. A knight named Walter de Leslin[41] and another knight named Livingus[42] would have fulfilled roles similar to Andreas's. George, the illegitimate son of Andrew I, likely seeking a fresh start in a place where his paternity would not be an issue, also joined the group. (In the Epilogue, I include short articles about these families.) The knights would have been able to set up and pack up camp at locations if the group could not find overnight lodging. Women and children would likely have been part of the traveling group also, at least the wives, as we know that de Leslin brought his son named Barthlomew.[43] There would have been at least several families, making a sizable group of people. Since everyone in this group was moving with any possessions that they valued, and their children, the travel across Europe to England would have been slow, probably requiring months. But everyone was willing to put up with some hardship, as they expected a rich windfall in England once Edward became king.

Top: Margaret, age about 11, Christina, age about 8 -
Front: Edward the Exile, Agatha and Edgar, age about 6.
Used by kind permission of Mary McKnight & family. created by kirsten reed

Edgar Aethling

Finally, we reach the subject of this book. As a boy of five or six years old in 1056–7, when the royal family set out to go to England, the young boy Edgar was at an age where he would be able to remember his home in Hungary and at least the highlights of the long trip to England. These are the first memories that Edgar would have to keep with him for a lifetime.

I can imagine that at the beginning of the journey to England, Edgar was possibly the most excited young boy who ever lived. A boy of that age is prone to adoring his father, and Edgar's father was going to England to sit next to the current king of England, Edward the Confessor. Then Edgar's father would become king! And someday, the lad would follow his father to become king!

The journey from Hungary to England alone would have been a memory that would have been burned into the mind of a small boy such as Edgar. The group was to cross the English Channel on a boat, which would be another new and amazing experience for those who had possibly never traveled far from Hungary. The travelers—our royal family and especially Edgar—would have been wide-eyed with excitement by the time they reached their destination.

However, they had only two days to enjoy England before Edward suddenly died. He was almost certainly assassinated. It is possible that Edward may have been a bit naive, not aware of the politics of his new environment, and too trusting of the men he found in England. He had lived the first several months of, and the last two days of, his life in what was supposed to be his home country. It is noteworthy that Edward was prevented from ever meeting King Edward the Confessor. The date of Edward's death is shown as April 19, 1057. The place of his death is London.[44]

Once again, Edward the Confessor was left without an heir to the throne within his family. Within England, Harold Godwinson[45] was the most prominent of several men who may have been considering their chance to become king once Edmund was out of the way. We have already noted that Edward had already given his promise to William, Duke of Normandy, that the latter would succeed him as king. Also, the Vikings still felt that they should be on the English throne. In other words, there was no shortage of men who could have been behind Edward's assassination.

The news and commentary of the day reflected the English people's feelings of sadness and disappointment. *The Anglo-Saxon Chronicle* of AD 1057 reported the following:

> This year came Edward Etheling, son of King Edmund, to this land, and soon after died. His body is buried within St. Paul's minster at London. He was brother's son to King

> Edward. King Edmund was called Ironside for his valour. This etheling King Knute had sent into Hungary, to betray him; but he there grew in favour with good men, as God granted him, and it well became him; so that he obtained the emperor's cousin in marriage, and by her had a fair offspring. Her name was Agatha. We know not for what reason it was done, that he should see his relation, King Edward. Alas! that was a rueful time, and injurious to all this nation—that he ended his life so soon after he came to England, to the misfortune of this miserable people.[46]

While the chronicle writer expressed sadness, I can scarcely imagine the feelings that Edgar experienced at this time. I imagine him thinking and saying:

"I will remember this moment forever. It started with some confusion. Several men were running. I walked down the path to the room where my father had been in a meeting. Looking in, I saw Father on the floor. Why is my father asleep on the floor? I wondered. The men appeared to be trying to wake him. Then one of the men whispered something to my mother. Dead? I was still small. This was my first memory of death. I began to weep. For a long time after that day, I continued to weep. My mother and Margaret and Christina would slap me and order me to stop crying, but I could not stop. I was just a little boy. I loved my father. The hours and days continued, but for me life seemed frozen like ice."

Edgar, and indeed the whole family, including Agatha, Margaret, and Christina, would have felt devastated. The families that had traveled from Hungary together would have been deeply disappointed. Edward was their pass to a rich life in England, but now he was lost. In today's times, we would say that this event was a huge psychological shock to the family. Grief counseling would ensue. Friends and associates from all over would pour out sympathy to the family. But in the eleventh century, death was not uncommon for people at any age, as medical care was almost nonexistent. The only possible comfort or consolation to the royal family that I can conceive of is that they would have been differently and better prepared by their conditioning to accept tragedy than a twenty-first-century family would be.

What would have happened to this royal family at this point? The written history does not mention Edgar again until 1066. But it seems that the royal family and their knights and servants were undeterred by the tragedy. Agatha, Margaret, Christina, Edgar, and, apparently, the entire group from Hungary stayed in England and became an extended part of the royal court of Edward the Confessor.

For the next nine years while Edgar was growing up, he would have enjoyed the royal life in England. His education would have been the best possible. He learned to read and write in the English language. He studied counting and arithmetic.

Edward began to mentor the young boy Edgar. The latter would have learned the history of England, especially the heroic defense of London led by Edmund Ironsides, his grandfather. Edward and older men would impress him with stories they recalled about fighting the Vikings and the kings Cnut, Harold, and Harthacnut. These men could even remember Edgar's great-grandfather Aethelred.

Edgar read the Bible and learned the most common stories from the Scriptures. He attended Mass often, likely every day, at the largest and most prominent churches in England. This brought him into contact with Latin, which may have become another subject for him to study.

Edgar would have dined with Edmund the Confessor occasionally and learned all about the politics of the time. He would have met Harold Godwinson and the other prominent noblemen of England. And since Edmund had connections to Normandy, the Aethelings may have even traveled there to meet William the Duke of Normandy and his sons. As Edgar was learning to become a king, he enjoyed all of the privileges of royalty. But while Edward the Confessor made promises, he failed to secure Edgar's, or anyone's, future in the line of succession. In Edgar's case, his young age and maturity, or lack thereof, may have been the problem.

Edgar's mother, Agatha, and his older sisters, Margaret and Christina, stayed in the royal court in England and learned from Edward the Confessor. Edgar may have suffered from being the younger brother of the family. But the family and the loyal Hungarians continued to learn and build upon the spiritual influences of their lives in Hungry.

The Duke of Normandy

William the Duke of Normandy was married to a woman named Matilda.[47] At the time, the couple were starting their own family. Their first son, named Robert Curthose,[48] was born between 1051 and 1054; he was very close in age to Edgar. Robert and Edgar would become lifelong friends. William and Matilda's second son was William Rufus,[49] born in 1056, and their third son was Henry,[50] born in 1068. Edgar would also likely have known William as a friend, but Robert was closer to him in age.

Malcolm Canmore

In the Confessor's court, there also came a young man in exile from Scotland named Malcolm Canmore,[51] a man who had a claim to the throne of Scotland. Edward the Confessor was at least trying to have some fun when he tried to set up Edgar's sister Margaret with Malcolm. But if Malcolm met Margaret at all during this time (1057), it would have been a very brief encounter. The news arrived from Scotland that a man named Lulach[52] had overthrown Macbeth[53](yes, the Macbeth of the famous Shakespeare play) as king of Scotland. But Lulach would reign for only months, as Malcolm, with the help of the English, was able to oust Lulach early in 1058. Malcolm would become known as Malcolm III. He married a Norwegian woman named Ingebjorg.[54] Their first son was Duncan,[55] born in 1060. Later, they would add two sons—Malcolm and Donald—and a daughter to their family.

The Year 1066

The events of this year had their origins in the time between Christmas and New Year's Eve in 1065 when Edward the Confessor fell ill. As New Year's Day passed, it became apparent to observers that Edward was on his deathbed. As he was failing, Edward was able to whisper that he wanted his longtime ally and closest adviser Harold Godwinson to succeed him as king. This would have made Harold at least the fourth man to whom Edward had given some sort promise in regards to succession (the first three were William, Duke of Normandy, Edward the Exile, and Edgar). Edward passed on January 5. Much later, Edward was later canonized as a saint in the Roman Catholic Church.

On January 6, the Witenagemot assembled and ratified Edmund's dying wish to install Harold as the next king of England. By far the most important consideration was that Harold would be a much more effective military leader than Edgar or anyone else. They already feared that William, Duke of Normandy, might attack. And even though almost twenty-four years had gone by since Harthacnut was king, the Vikings still claimed the English throne for Denmark and Sweden. Obviously, the men in the Witenagemot regarded the Duke of Normandy as an unwelcome foreigner whom they did not want to be king. Nor were they inclined to select Edgar.

Edgar would have been about fifteen years old at this time, making him older than Edward the Martyr and Aethelred had been when they were chosen king, but there is a disturbing clue about Edgar's maturity in the historical narrative. *The Anglo-Saxon Chronicle* refers to Edgar as "the child Edgar."[56] I certainly would not expect a young person of Edgar's age(about 15) to be described with such a critical term as this, especially not in the rough and hard-to-survive Middle Ages. Was something wrong with Edgar?

I would speculate that upon the death of his father, Edgar could not help but take upon himself a deep emotional hurt, one that continued to bother him as he grew. Perhaps he could not communicate very well and acted younger than his age. While Edgar should have had a number of male role models to follow, his family life, with only his mother and two older sisters giving him orders, may have hampered his development into manhood.

On the other hand, it was apparent that the leaders of the Witan felt that Harold's experience would be an advantage. Was Edgar angry or disappointed by this decision? Or was he somehow able to accept this judgment? This decision did seem to put an end to the rule of the House of Wessex, as Harold had other family members who could follow him, thereby leaving Edgar bereft of any further claim to the throne.

This was just the beginning of what would become a very turbulent year for England. William the Duke of Normandy felt that he was first in line, as the promise that he received from Edward went all the way back to 1051. Obviously, the Witan were unimpressed by Edward's friendly gesture and wanted nothing to do with the Normans. In response, William was going to go to war to gain what he felt was rightfully his.

It took William all spring and summer to assemble a suitable army and a navy with enough boats to transport his forces to England. As the prevailing winds were unfavorable, William's forces were forced to wait in Normandy. But in this delay, William actually had good fortune on his side.

In September, the Vikings, under the king of Norway, Harald Hardrada,[57] landed in England. Harold Godwinson's own brother, Earl Tostig,[58] had actually accompanied the Norwegians and brought some of his own armed force. Two English earls, Morcar and Edwin, lived in the north of England and commanded an English army. On September 20, this army was beaten by the Norwegians. But Harold was already on the way with his army to meet the invaders. On September 25, the English routed the Norwegians in the Battle of Stamford Bridge.[59] Harald Hardrada and Earl Tostig were both killed, and the remaining invaders fled to their ships. But the English army had taken some serious casualties as well, and emerged as a weakened force.

William probably had not even heard news of the Stamford Bridge battle when the winds finally changed in favor of the Normans. Only three days later, on September 28, William crossed the English Channel and landed his force near Hastings. This was stunning news to King Harold. He now needed to quickly reassemble his army and travel to meet the new threat. Moving the army the large distance from Stamford Bridge to Hastings alone would be a daunting task. The English army was still not at its full strength when, on October 14, the Norman and English forces came together near the village of Hastings.

The Battle of Hastings[60] must be described as one of the most desperate battles of all of history. The Normans knew that they would be massacred on the beach if they did not hold their line. The English knew that they would remain an independent country if they prevailed, as they had already defeated the Vikings. The battle soon became a war of attrition, with both sides suffering enormous casualties. There is a legend that King Harold was struck by an arrow directly in his eye but continued to fight until he was killed. The king's brothers, Earl Gurth and Earl Leofwin, were also killed. The battle lasted all day, then the Normans began to retreat. But this was a deception, one that caused the English army to break ranks and pursue the Normans. With the English forces spread out, a fierce Norman counterattack prevailed. The English army collapsed and retreated. The Normans under Duke William claimed the victory.

There is a fascinating cloth known as the Bayeux Tapestry[61] that shows in needlepoint historic scenes from the history of this time and the Battle at Hastings.

Where would Edgar have been while these Battles of Stamford Bridge and Hastings were raging? It seems unlikely that he would have been involved in the fighting at his age, although it is possible that a young man of sixteen could have fought. Would he have watched these battles from a distance? Or was he sequestered safely in London?

The news of the loss of King Harold caused the Witenagemot to reassemble. On the next day, October 15, Edgar was named the king of England. So finally we have answered the question as to how Edgar became the king of England. Edgar had reached the position he believed was his destiny!

Edgar was supported by the most powerful remaining English leaders: Stigand, Archbishop of Canterbury; Ealdred, Archbishop of York; Edwin, Earl of Mercia; and Morcar, Earl of Northumbria. What would Edgar's mood be like now? With King Harold dead and the English army defeated, I can envision a room full of very worried men. Perhaps Edgar felt their sense of impending doom. What decisions would he make during his reign? Or could Edgar have allowed himself some slight wave of excitement when looking at the crown of the king of England? Every king looks forward to his coronation ceremony. When would Edgar's coronation ceremony take place?

As it turns out, Edgar never would be crowned king. Apparently, the men surrounding Edgar felt that a coronation ceremony would further provoke William and place Edgar in greater danger. William, who was now known as "the Conqueror," ordered his army to advance into England. The English army, having lost at Hastings, was still providing some armed resistance, but this was insufficient to stop the Normans, who were now advancing toward London. The Norman army was now able to pillage and loot whatever they cared to take. Negotiations started between William and several of the prominent English landowners. Could William be satisfied with having control of part of England, as the compromise had been with the Vikings in 1016? Could England be a separate state under his protection?

But William had won the battle and had no need of any compromise. Archbishop Stigand met secretly with William, and the two agreed on a peace agreement. When other prominent landowners learned of Stigand's agreement, they also met with William to offer their submission. On December 8, Edgar was brought to William at Berkhampstead Castle.[62] *The Anglo-Saxon Chronicle* of AD 1066 reported as follows:

> He [William] came to Berkhampstead; where Archbishop Aldred came to meet him, with child Edgar, and Earls Edwin and Morkar, and all the best men from London; who submitted then for need, when the most harm was done. It was very ill-advised that they did not so before, seeing that God would not better things for our sins. And they gave him hostages and took oaths: and he promised them that he would be a faithful lord to them; though in the midst of this they plundered wherever they went.[63]

A difficult moment for Edgar: He must abdicate his position as the King. Emotionally, he must accept a strange and foreign authority figure. Physically, he even had to look up at the taller William. *Westbow Press Illustration*

Thus, Edgar was forced to abdicate after acting as king for fifty-four days. William would be the king of all of England and Normandy combined. The best that Edgar could do was to manage a good face to hide his true feelings. England had known four kings in the calendar year 1066. The conflict and economic turmoil would continue for several years, but eventually the new leadership would provide stability.

William the Conqueror

The Duke of Normandy now had added the nickname "the Conqueror" to his list of titles. Actually, William was not entirely the "foreign" invader that some may have perceived him to be. As we have seen, in the complex family relationships of the royalty, William was yet another relative to the English royal family, as he was related to Emma, the mother of Edward the Confessor. But William was French, and that was not welcomed by the English.

William actually tried to accommodate Edgar as much as he could. By making Edgar, as well as Agatha, Margaret, Christina, and their friends, part of his royal court, he could salve the lingering anger of the English people. If Edgar could appear to support the decision making, then William would gain favor in the minds of the English public. On Christmas Day 1066, likely with Edgar, Agatha, Margaret, and Christina watching, William's coronation ceremony was held. William received the crown of the king of England. William picked Christmas Day to celebrate as it had been exactly fifty years to the day since Cnut the Viking had been crowned king of England, so they purposefully made that the day, in order to mark a new start.

Our royal family, and likely the loyal Hungarians, stayed in the company of William the Conqueror long enough to travel with him back to Normandy in 1067. *The Anglo-Saxon Chronicle* of AD 1067 reported, "William traveled at Lent and went over sea to Normandy, taking with him Archbishop Stigand, and Abbot Aylnoth of Glastonbury, and the child Edgar, and the Earls Edwin, Morkar, and Waltheof, and many other good men of England."[64] This group of people began to learn the ways and customs of the Normans. I suspect, however, that the Aethelings and some of their Hungarian friends found the Normans to be carnal and worldly, lacking in the exceptional spiritual qualities that the former had been accustomed to in Hungary and when under Edward the Confessor.

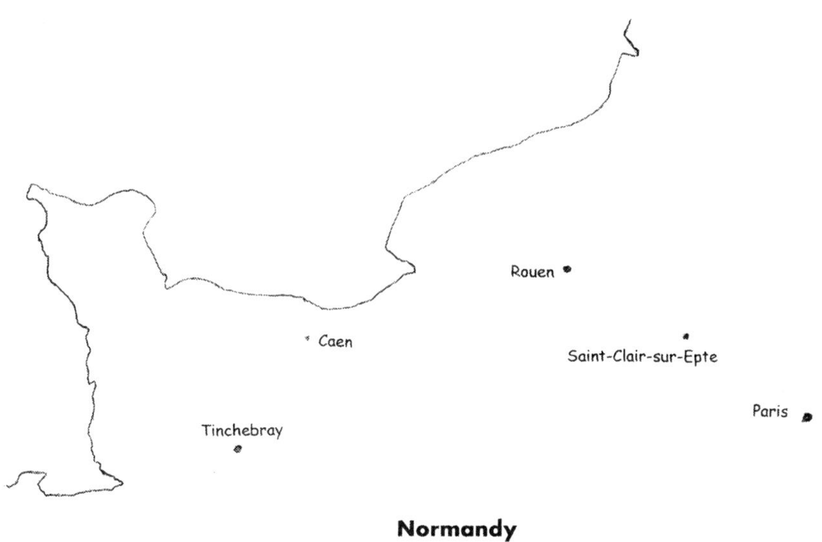

Normandy

William ruled Normandy and England from his home in Rouen.

The Anglo-Saxon Chronicle mentions that Earl Leofric, Abbot of Peterborough, also traveled with the group to Normandy, but he became ill and died upon returning to England.

> The monks then chose for abbot Provost Brand [to replace Leofric], because he was a very good man, and very wise; and sent him to Edgar Etheling, for that the land-folk supposed that he [Edgar] should be king: and the Etheling received him gladly. When King William heard say that, he was very wroth [this appeared to be a rebellion], and said that the abbot had renounced him: but good men went between them, and reconciled them; because the abbot was a good man. He [the abbot] gave the king forty marks of gold for his reconciliation.[65]

Thus, Edgar avoided being associated with the rebellion. However, most English people suffered, as it would be several years before a sense of normalcy could return to the country. The economy suffered when King William imposed a heavy tax. Even worse, some of his men continued to plunder parts of England when they could take advantage of the lawless conditions. The war even continued, as the Normans had to lay siege to the city of Exeter before overcoming its defenses. The Normans were beginning to assert their French style of feudalism and culture in England, but the English people were not readily going to accept the new order. One history source notes that before 1066 England was in the Dark Ages, but after 1066 England entered the Middle Ages. It is doubtless that many English people felt their freedoms being eroded by the more organized culture of feudalism.

To help William settle his new possession, England, and provide a reward, a number of men were "granted lands by Duke William of Normandy, their liege Lord, for their distinguished assistance at the battle of Hastings in 1066 A.D."[66] Some of these men eventually went to Scotland and became part of the Scottish clan system (a close association of relatives and other neighboring family clans).

To Scotland

Later in the year 1067, after some discussion, the royal family and their friends determined that for the cause of their freedom they should leave the court of the Conqueror. They rejected the idea of simply returning to Hungary and forgetting all about their last ten-plus years of misfortune in England. Our royal family and their court set sail from Normandy into the North Sea and soon found themselves swept up in a fierce storm that carried them north. They made it to shore at Wearmouth on the eastern coast of England. Upon returning to England, they found that some people were still fighting a rebellion against the Normans. They also got a clue that they might be able to find an ally in Scotland. Was God using the storm to lead them that way? After repairing their ship, they continued to sail north to Scotland. Their ship sailed past Edinburgh and landed on the north side of the Firth of Forth near Dunfermline. This landing site was later named St. Margaret's Hope("St. Margaret's Hope" now refers to a location in the Orkney Islands). Landing near Dunfermline would have been intentional, as this was the location of the royal residence. King of Scotland Malcolm Canmore quickly came to greet the new arrivals.

Malcolm would become a very receptive and willing ally, willing to help Edgar regain the English throne.

Edgar the Outlaw

There were several major battles in the rebellion. The following is from *The Anglo-Saxon Chronicle,* AD 1068.

> This year King William gave Earl Robert the earldom over Northumberland; but the landsmen attacked him in the town of Durham, and slew him, and nine hundred men with him. Soon afterwards Edgar Etheling came with all the Northumbrians to York; and the townsmen made a treaty with him: but King William came from the South unawares on them with a large army, and put them to flight, and slew on the spot those who could not escape; which were many hundred men; and plundered the town. St. Peter's minster he made a profanation, and all other places also he despoiled and trampled upon; and the etheling [Edgar] went back again to Scotland.[67]

The Northumbrians still believed that they could remain independent, but William was not going to tolerate a rebellion anywhere in England. The unlucky Edgar missed the victory, arriving only in time to retreat.

Edgar now was given the nickname "Edgar the Outlaw" for his part in becoming at least the figurehead leader of the rebellion. Certainly this name would have been quite offensive to Edgar and his family.

In 1069, King William named Earl Waltheof, Earl of Northumberland, as the replacement for Earl Robert. This was another unlucky appointment, as William did not realize that Waltheof was actually a third cousin to both King Sweyn II of Denmark[68] and King Harold II of England, who had been killed at Hastings. In late summer, a fleet of 240 ships led by 3 of the sons of King Sweyn II came from Denmark and sailed into the Humber River,

> where they met with Child Edgar, the Atheling, the rightful King of England and Earl Walthcof and Mcrlc Swcync,

> and Earl Gospatric with the Northumbrians, and all the landsmen; riding and marching full merrily with an immense army: and so all advanced to York; where they stormed and demolished the castle, and won innumerable treasures therein; slew there many hundreds of Frenchmen.[69]

Edgar arrives after the battle is over. Even though he is only about 18 years old, he leads an attack on the Normans. Here are Edgar's thoughts after the next action:

"How amazing is this; the Vikings are my allies! Just a few years ago we, the English, had defeated the Vikings, but now we welcome their return. The men of Northumberland consider the Vikings to be their brothers and are now united in my cause; to rid our land of the hated Normans. The combined army we now have will outnumber the Normans, we will yet retrace our steps to Hastings, and cast the conqueror into the sea. Our first battle was over before I had even arrived; we retake York, killing many Normans, retrieving our money and destroying the castle. Now I will press our advantage. By sea I will lead my elite force on a raid further south from York. But then, disaster strikes. My group of raiders reaches a much larger Norman army than we expected. Most of my men are lost, only a few men and myself are able to escape to rejoin our main army. A must: I must outnumber the enemy. I miss my men, but I must remember that the men are unimportant, they are just stepping stones to reach my rightful place as king of England, just as men are unimportant to William and other leaders. Then when I am alone, I cry again. I have lost men. A demon is following me. Somehow I must strengthen myself to become a man."[70]

Once again, William had to react to losing York:

> When the king [William] heard this, then he went northward with all the force that he could collect, despoiling and laying waste all the shire withal [York, Northumberland]; whilst this fleet [of the Danes] lay all winter in the Humber [mouth of the river] where the King could not get at them."[71]

Early in 1070, William was able to negotiate with the Danes. He paid them to leave England. With York once again controlled by the Normans, William's army pursued Edgar and the remaining rebels toward Scotland, where Malcolm could provide shelter.

Invasion of 1072

Malcolm and Edgar had enough armed forces to harass the English and Normans wherever they could. Northumberland, the area between England and Scotland, was sparsely populated and had become a nearly lawless frontier. Malcolm had discovered that captured Englishmen could be forced into slavery; thus, he had developed a penchant for raiding and attacking England. King William had been pushing his army north from York through Northumberland. By 1072, they had reached Scotland. But Malcolm made an unusually wise decision not to fight the stronger Norman–English forces. The forces agreed to negotiate, and Malcolm accepted stringent terms: he had to recognize William in England, and he had to turn over his twelve-year-old son Duncan to the English as a hostage. It was likely that many of the English slaves, when they could be found, were returned. But the land area of Scotland and Northumberland was far too vast for the Norman–English army, given their size and their limited weapons, to control. Malcolm was humbled, but he was allowed to continue to rule Scotland. Edgar left Scotland and traveled to Flanders, the land area north of Normandy. It is uncertain, but Edgar's going from Scotland into exile yet again may have been a requirement of the peace agreement.[72]

Shipwrecked

In 1074, Edgar returned to Scotland. King Malcolm(who had by now married Edgar's sister Margaret) greeted him "with much pomp," possibly meaning a parade and a celebration. Then Edgar heard of another opportunity.

> [Edgar] received an offer from king Phillip I of France who was also opposed to William, of a castle and lands near the border of Normandy from which he would be able to raid his enemies homeland. Edgar embarked with his followers for France, but a storm wrecked their ships on the English coast. Many of Edgar's men were hunted down by the Normans, but he managed to escape with the remainder to Scotland. Following this disaster, Edgar was persuaded by Malcolm to make peace with William and return to England as his subject, abandoning any ambition of regaining his ancestral throne.[73]

The Anglo-Saxon Chronicle adds that Malcolm and Margaret provided Edgar and his men many presents and treasures, but these were almost all lost in the shipwreck.

Peace

Perhaps the ever-prayerful Margaret persuaded Edgar to believe that the storm was another device God was using to change the direction of Edgar's life. Even Malcolm had no desire to continue fighting. *The Anglo-Saxon Chronicle* from the year AD 1074 reads as follows:

> Then King Malcolm advised [Edgar] to send to King William over sea, to request his friendship, which he did; and the king gave it him, and sent after him. Again, therefore, King Malcolm and his sister gave him and all his men numberless treasures, and again conducted him very magnificently from their territory. The sheriff of York came to meet him at Durham, and went all the way with him; ordering meat and fodder to be found for him at every castle to which they came, until they came over sea to the king. Then King William received him with much pomp; and he was there afterwards in his court, enjoying such rights as he confirmed to him by law.[74]

This kind treatment provided to Edgar, the loser of the rebellion against King William, by all of those people who were around him shows how very much King William desired to avoid further bloodshed. Edgar was worth much more alive than dead if Edgar's support could smooth over the rough feelings aroused by the Norman conquest.

William actually traveled to England only on very rare occasions while he ruled, preferring to remain in Normandy. Obviously, William felt much safer in Normandy. For the next ten years, we read nothing more about Edgar. He likely remained in Normandy most, if not all, of that time serving in William's court, although it certainly seems possible that he would have visited his family in Scotland and traveled to England on occasions. During this time in Normandy, Edgar also developed his relationships with the sons of William the Conqueror. His best friend was William's first son, Robert Curthose, as Edgar was about three years older than Robert. Best of all, Edgar was paid to be loyal and to do nothing, although the latter could hardly be a fulfilling occupation. But William might have been best advised to leave Edgar in Scotland. I imagine Edgar saying to Robert:

"Listen, Robert, you should take the lead in this, to overthrow your father. You shall be the Duke of Normandy, and I shall return to my place as king of England. How about that?"

I see Robert's reply: ***"Edgar, I think you are right. The people in England do not like my father. I can become more than a duke; I shall be the king of Normandy. Together we will be more effective than my father alone, and we will be much richer."***

By 1079, Robert had gained enough support in Normandy and France to form a rebellion against his father. This resulted in a battle at Castle Gerboyor. The violent attack wounded even the Conqueror and his second son, William Rufus. King William noted his first son's behavior and was not pleased. In the future, this would cost Robert.

Margaret

The fame of Edgar's oldest sister, Margaret, actually greatly exceeds Edgar's very slight place in history. Margaret's story adds deep dimensions of family, Christian faith, and character to our understanding of Edgar's life.

The Anglo-Saxon Chronicle for the year AD 1067 (sometimes the chronicle of an event wasn't written until several years had passed, so the entry below likely appeared many years later) reads as follows:

> This summer the child Edgar departed, with his mother Agatha, and his two sisters, Margaret and Christina, and Merle-Sweyne [Merle-Sweyne was born in England and was related to the Viking King Sweyne of Denmark], and many *good men* [surely this refers to the Hungarians who had journeyed with Edward the Exile and perhaps some others from England] with them; and came to Scotland under the protection of King Malcolm, who entertained them all. Then began King Malcolm to yearn after the child's [Edgar's] sister, Margaret, to wife [a remarkable statement to include in a historical document]; but he [Edgar] and all his men long refused; and she also herself was averse, and said that she would neither have him nor any one else, if the Supreme Power would grant, that she in her maidenhood might please the mighty Lord with a carnal heart, in this short life, in pure continence. The king, however, earnestly urged her brother [Edgar], until he answered Yea. And indeed he durst not otherwise; for they were come into his kingdom. So that then it was fulfilled, as God had long ere foreshowed; and else it could not be; as he himself saith in his gospel: that "not even a sparrow on the ground may fall, without his foreshowing." The prescient Creator wist long before what he of her would have done; for that she should increase the glory of God in this land, lead the king aright from the path of error, bend him and his people together to a better way, and suppress the bad customs which the nation formerly followed: all which she afterwards did.[75]

Malcolm was married to Ingebjorg when Margaret and the Aethelings had arrived, but apparently Ingebjorg had died in 1069, so Malcolm was single again. The facts that Margaret made it to Scotland in late 1067 and that Ingebjorg passed one or two years later is enough for me to cast some suspicion on the ruthless Malcolm concerning what may have happened to Ingebjorg.

It was 1070 when Malcolm and Margaret were married. This marriage offended William the Conqueror, as it provided credibility to Edgar's claim to the throne of England. This may have offered another justification of the 1072 invasion of Scotland.

For Malcolm, it was love at first sight. For Margaret, getting married was her duty. *Westbow Press Illustration*

The couple eventually had eight children. In order of birth, these children are as follows: five boys, Edward (c. 1071), Edmund,[76] (c. 1072), Ethelred (c. 1074), Edgar[77] (c. 1075), and Alexander[78] (c. 1078); then two girls, Edith[79] (c. 1080) and Mary[80] (1082); and then one more son, David[81](c. 1083). Obviously, the couple employed servants to help take care of such a group. We know that Christina, who was serving as a nun, was also involved in the child care, especially mentoring the two girls. The fact that all of these children grew to adulthood is a considerable achievement in itself, given the state of medical care at that time.

Soon, the energetic Margaret began to influence the entire nation of Scotland. In Europe, Benedictine monasteries were common. When Margaret found that there were no Benedictine monasteries in Scotland, she invited some Benedictine monks to establish new monasteries in the country. One of the Benedictine monks was a man named Turgot, who developed a close friendship with Margaret. He eventually wrote a biography of Margaret, at the request of Margaret's daughter Edith, after the latter had become the queen of England in 1100. Writing about her Christian faith and character, Turgot commented as follows:

> Whilst Margaret was yet in the flower of youth, she began to lead a very strict life, to love God above all things, to employ herself in the study of the Divine writings, and therein with joy to exercise her mind. Her understanding was keen to comprehend any matter, whatever it might be; to this was joined a great tenacity of memory, enabling her to store it up, along with a graceful flow of language to express it.[82]

As you can see, Turgot was very grateful to, and easily lavished praise upon, Margaret. But we can also be sure that Margaret was extremely bright, had a charismatic personality, and had the ability to communicate effectively. Margaret applied her Christian faith and her considerable intellect to bringing several major reforms to Scotland.

In addition to establishing monasteries, Margaret found that some churches in Scotland were missing some of the basic practices of Christianity. She was able to persuade people to change the Scottish church to conform more closely in worship to the larger Roman Catholic Church. This corrected worship practices and promoted unity within the church.

As the royal residence was located in Dunfermline, Margaret soon started a church close by in the town. This church was known then as the Church of the Holy Trinity. Today it the Dunfermline Abbey.[83] Margaret also found a large stone and a cave in almost the same place near Dunfermline. The stone appeared to be like a seat along the road. On the stone, she would frequently sit and speak freely with anyone who wished; thus, access to her was very easy. The location of this stone even came to be marked on maps as St. Margaret's Stone.[84] Margaret would also frequently retreat into the cave. She used the cave as a place to study her devotions, pray, and fast, although I would certainly think that most of her fasting came after her lengthy childbearing years. The cave is marked on maps as St. Margaret's Cave.[85]

To help provide for people, Margaret frequently opened up the family castle home to feed and entertain homeless people, poor people, and children—an activity almost unheard of for a head of state. Turgot also mentions that Margaret would pillage coins from Malcolm, sometimes even taking Malcolm's coins from the church offering plate, and give them to the needy. Turgot believed that Malcolm would either pretend not to notice or act amused when he did notice.

Margaret came to have a huge influence on Scotland, as Malcolm would often seek her advice on affairs of state. With the help of the other English and Hungarian exiles, the Scottish government was reformed to conform more closely to English and European systems.

Margaret, the Aethelings, and our exiles (Andreas, Walter de Leslin, Livingus, and others) also wakened Scotland to art and education from the Continent. The new ideas and styles were well received by the Scots. English and European merchants benefited from the increased trade and communication with the Scottish.

When Malcolm and Margaret met with Scottish people, Margaret would speak English and Malcolm would frequently translate her speech to the native Gaelic language. As the Scots began to recognize the benefits of a common language with England, Margaret's influence caused Scotland to change its official language from Gaelic to English. In all of the history of humankind, I believe that this is one of the few occurrences when the people of a nation willingly changed their spoken language. Today, all of Scotland knows and uses English. Gaelic is still used as a second language, but this only among a small part of the population in the far northern and western areas of Scotland.

In one instance, Margaret, in her kindness, worked at cross-purposes with Malcolm. In the midst of the on-again, off-again conflicts between the English and the Scots, a number of Englishmen had been taken prisoner and were pressed into service as slaves in Scotland. The Scots occasionally sent raids into Northumberland to try to capture more men to be used as slaves. In fact, Malcolm himself often led the raiding party. Malcolm came to be regarded as a hated barbarian to the English in Northumberland. Eventually, his raids became his undoing. But Margaret kept a number of contacts in Scotland who informed her of where these prisoners were being held. Once they were found, Margaret paid a ransom to have them set them free, probably using money that Malcolm had just placed in the church offering plate.

When Malcolm and Margaret were together, she would read the Bible to him, as he had not learned to read or write. Malcolm would kiss the Bible when Margaret was finished reading. Malcolm also had Margaret's Bible and other books decorated with gold and gems. The contrast couldn't be more stark: the warrior Malcolm led attacks on England in 1061, 1068–72, 1079, 1091, and 1093, and took captives to be used as slaves, but he also worshiped gently with his devout wife. Malcolm and Margaret were certainly one of history's most unlikely couples, but their success together and their descendants had a lasting and profound effect on Scotland.

The Holyrood

When Margaret traveled to Scotland, she was in possession of an incredible artifact that came to be called the Holyrood, also the Black Cross. It is thought that Margaret had brought this piece all the way from Hungary.[86] It is possible that this cross may have handed down to her. But if it was not inherited, then Margaret would have instructed the craftsmen as to how her design for this cross should be completed even before she had reached her teenage years.

The name Black Cross came from the black case that held the object, as the case could be opened and closed like a chest. The chest and the cross contained within it were made in a simple cross shape of equal lengths, not in the cross shape of the crucifix. The Black Cross was described in various ways, from wood to pure gold, and was set with diamonds and possibly other gems. On the cross was some section, or at least some small length of wood, that was supposed to have come from the very cross that was used to crucify Christ. Also there was an ivory crucifix attached to the top of the cross. Here is another description:

"The Black Cross itself was of gold, and set with large diamonds. It is about an ell long, … manufactured in pure gold, of most wonderful workmanship, and may be shut and opened like a chest. Inside is seen a portion of our Lord's Cross (as has often been proved by convincing miracles), having a figure of our Saviour sculptured out of massive ivory, and marvelously adorned with gold."[88]

Margaret could captivate a group of people when describing the Holyrood. *Westbow Press Illustration*

An ell is a unit of measurement that represents the distance from a man's elbow to the tip of his middle finger, about 18 inches (46 cm). However, in various countries, this measurement, as well as the double ell, came to indicate a variety of distances that ranged from about 24 inches to more than 54 inches (61 to 137 cm), thus leaving us quite uncertain about how to determine the actual size. For the purpose of creating our illustration, I decided that the overall size of the cross should be about 27 inches (about 69 cm), which is approximately the length of the ell according to the measurement systems of several European countries in that time period.[88]

Margaret kept this cross close to her at virtually all times, and she used it for her own personal devotions. It certainly would have made quite an impression on her audience any time that she used it to aid her missionary efforts.

The actual history of this artifact and the source of the wood that was used to make it seemed to be unknown prior to Margaret's possession of the cross. There is historic evidence that the True Cross, or what was thought to be the True Cross, may well have had numerous small pieces of wood taken from it and distributed widely so that more people could see it. Thus, descriptions of this artifact all treat the small length of wood used on its front as authentic—i.e., as being part of the cross upon which Christ was crucified. Eventually, the Holyrood became a family heirloom to Malcolm and Margaret's sons and an icon for Scotland. The couple's youngest son, David, became king in 1124. He built a large church to house the cross, naming the church the Holyrood.

Italy

We learn that Edgar cashed out much of his fortune and took approximately two hundred knights with him to Italy in 1085, as a group of Normans were determined to establish themselves in Sicily and southern Italy.[89] What would Edgar and his knights do there?

I can imagine them laying on the beach, drinking wine, and trying to find women whom they could persuade to enjoy their company. That is my "simple" thought. Or Edgar's knights could have served as an honor guard at the Vatican while Edgar sought an appointment from the pope. This latter is a more "noble" idea, but I do not consider Rome to be located in southern Italy.

More realistically, Edgar and his knights may have fought in some battles, as the Normans had undertaken an invasion to conquer the area of southern Italy. This conflict had started around the year 1000 and would continue for another century; thus, it is probably better described as frontier settling than as a war.[90] But whatever Edgar and his knights did, their stay lasted only about eighteen months. And Edgar's stay in Italy was termed unsuccessful.[91]

Rebellion

News came to Edgar from Normandy that William the Conqueror had fallen from his horse. His internal injuries were sufficient to cause his death, which occurred about one week after the accident, in August of 1087. The struggle for the throne of Normandy and England was on again! This would have been sufficient reason for Edgar to leave Italy.

As William lay in pain, he declared that his first son, Robert Curthose, should not be granted the throne. This was William's reaction to the previous rebellions in which Robert had been involved. Thus, William's second son, known as William Rufus, ascended to the throne of England as William II. Although Robert inherited only part of Normandy, he was still considered to be the Duke of Normandy. Thus, William II would begin to reign in England, but he also would control part of Normandy. This was not how his father, who seldom left Normandy, ruled.

Robert, being about three years younger than Edgar, would have been Edgar's best friend among the sons of William the Conqueror. Feeling that he had been unfairly bypassed for the throne, and urged on by many of the nobility who thought that England and Normandy should stay united, Robert started an armed rebellion against his younger brother. Robert persuaded Edgar to join his rebellion. Edgar would be of great help to him, as Edgar could bring his knights into the conflict as well.

During this rebellion, Robert was able to control some land in Normandy that belonged to William II. Robert then parceled out this land to some of his followers, including Edgar. This division of land was short-lived, as William invaded Normandy in 1091 and, once he succeeded, forced Robert and Edgar to accept his terms. An agreement was reached to restore the land to William II and to the other, previous owners. The agreement reconciled Robert to his brother William II. However, Edgar was not included in the agreement. He returned to Scotland to once again ask the support of King Malcolm.

Malcolm was always ready to launch an attack. With the internal conflict in England suggesting English weakness, he launched another of his raids into Northumberland. William II responded by marching his army north into England. After the two forces confronted each other, their leaders finally made a reasonable decision to negotiate rather than shed blood over land that was far from where these two armies had met. Remarkably, Edgar negotiated on behalf of Malcolm with Robert, representing William II. The two friends soon reached a peaceful agreement. However, the treaty with Robert was not honored by William II. Within a few months, both Robert and Edgar left for Normandy to try to restart their rebellion. William II also did not honor the treaty with Malcolm. In 1093, Malcolm resumed his raids into England.[92]

November 1093

What occurred at this time was a course of events that, it would seem, only the writers of screenplays could invent. This is yet another amazing and very touching story. Margaret had fallen seriously ill at some time in this year. Margaret's biographer Turgot offered this opinion: "As for her fasting … the strictness of her abstinence brought upon her a very severe infirmity."[93] Of course, we have no way of knowing what caused her to suffer. Turgot indicated that Margaret's illness had persisted for at least six months. This would indicate that Margaret had an actual and serious illness with symptoms brought on by something other than fasting. In modern medical science, starvation from fasting can be a cause of death, which would occur in much less than six months after one stopped eating.[94] Certainly Margaret had the means to avoid starvation.

Turgot now wrote these chilling words: "It would seem that her [Margaret's] departure from this world, as well as certain other events which were impending, had been known by her long beforehand."[95] Privately, Margaret summoned Turgot to her bedside and, once he arrived, began to recount the history of her life. Turgot recalled that the emotion of the moment frequently overcame both of them. Margaret would begin to weep, then Turgot himself would also weep. Their shedding of tears was followed by lengthy periods of silence between them. Then, as Margaret prayed with a desperate intensity, Turgot recalled something else: "I heard the language of the Holy Ghost speaking* by her tongue."[96]

Turgot was startled by hearing this spiritual language. It left him deeply moved by Margaret's sincerity and kindness. Shortly after Margaret prayed, Turgot had to take his leave. The two then exchanged their final farewells to one another. Margaret was left in the care of a priest who later provided to Turgot more details of her last days.

Four days before Margaret's death, this priest noticed that Margaret became unusually sad. After the priest asked her how she was feeling, Margaret replied,

"Perhaps on this very day such a heavy calamity may befall the realm of Scotland as has not been for many ages past."[97]

---

* When I was a newly converted Christian many years ago, I attended a Methodist church, however, since as a child I had no church home, I felt comfortable enough visiting other worship services as a way of learning. I found a number of "Pentecostal meetings" where speaking in tongues occurred often. Sometimes there were people who were Roman Catholic, and considered themselves "Catholic Charismatics." Their explanation of spiritual gifts included the book of Acts, where the gift of speaking in tongues began, then ended, and now they teach that these gifts are reappearing as the world approaches the "last days" when the "spirit will be poured out" (Joel 2:28–29). However, on the other side of the issue there were some Baptists and more traditional Christians. Their preachers were certain that the gift of speaking in tongues ended in Apostolic times. I can actually recall several sermons critical of Pentecostals and warnings to not be involved in the Pentecostal movement. They considered the Pentecostals to be on the fringe of being Christians at all. But, obviously, neither of these theological points of view comprehended that the Queen of Scotland, in the midst of the middle ages, was indeed a such a charismatic. Thus I was surprised when I found this.

The priest remembered these words clearly but did not understand what they could mean until three days later, when a messenger arrived with news that Malcolm, Margaret's husband and king, and Edward, the couple's oldest son and the heir to the throne, had been together when they were killed. They had been at the head of another of their raids into England when they were surprised by an ambush near Alnwick[98] in Northumberland. This had indeed happened on the twelfth of November, the very same day as Margaret's episode of sadness. However, this news was kept from Margaret.

The next day, November 16, Margaret was able to attend Mass, but afterward the pain from her disease intensified. Sensing that her death was near, she asked for the Holyrood to be brought to her so that she may hold it one last time. Then Margaret's fourth son, Edgar[99] (however, the text of Turgot's writing seems to indicate that this was the second son, Edmund, as Turgot refers to the son "holding the reins of government," and as Edmund was the next son in succession), probably Margaret's favorite of her sons, arrived with the intention of telling Margaret the news of the tragedy that had happened. Having also been away with the army, he was stunned to find his mother in such poor health.

Upon seeing Edgar, Margaret was able to rally her strength one more time. She asked him about his father, Malcolm, and his brother Edward. Unwilling to cause his mother any more distress, Edgar replied that they were fine. However, Margaret was not reassured:

"But, with a deep sigh she exclaimed, 'I know it, my boy, I know it. By this holy cross, by the bond of our blood, I adjure you to tell me the truth.'

Thus pressed, he [Edgar] told her exactly all that had happened."[100] Incredibly, Margaret seemed to have had a supernatural vision of the events in her husband's and son's lives, as well as in her own.

Turgot now describes Margaret in terms similar to those used in the book of Job. "At the same moment she had lost her husband and her son, and disease was bringing her to a cruel death, yet in all these things she sinned not with her lips, nor spoke foolishly against God. Raising her eyes and her hands towards heaven, she glorified God."[101] Turgot describes Margaret's last words as a prayer, which, when she completed it with the words *Deliver me*, "her soul was freed from the chains of the body, and departed to Christ."[102]

Margaret was been between forty-seven and forty-nine years of age when she passed. Her body was placed in the church that she previously had built, the one known today as Dunfermline Abbey. Margaret, as well as several of her sons who became kings of Scotland, remain interred there. A chapel named for Margaret was built in the early 1100s at the castle in Edinburgh.[103] In the year 1250, Margaret was canonized as a saint in the Roman Catholic Church. Since then, several churches around the world have been named in her honor.

Chaos in the Scottish Monarchy

With the near simultaneous passings of Malcolm; his eldest son and designated successor, Edward; and Margaret, the Scottish monarchy lapsed into disorder. Edmund claimed to be the rightful king, but Malcolm's brother Donald Ban (or Bane), who had spent much of his life in exile in Ireland, also was able to exert his influence to gain a majority control of Scotland. He would become known as Donald III.[104] Edmund would control the southern part of Scotland. However, the conflict between Scotland and England seemed to continue, with Edmund's forces along the English border. William II in England was tired of war against Scotland, and now he saw a chance to change the direction of Scotland. Malcolm and Ingebjorg's son Duncan had been held hostage in England from 1072 until 1087. Following the death of William the Conqueror, Robert Curthose released Duncan. By this time, Duncan's life was now prospering; he had married and had one son. But with his father Malcolm, now dead, he found a new opportunity to be a leader. William II also seized this chance and had Duncan named the figurehead leader of an English army. When this force invaded Scotland, Duncan was able to oust Donald and Edmund. He named himself king and become known as Duncan II.[105] However, many people in Scotland viewed Duncan as someone who had become an Englishman and who was an invader. This resentment boiled over and quickly began to strain the political leadership in Scotland. Duncan was able to reign for only several months during 1094 before he was assassinated by a regional governor. Duncan's assassination allowed Donald and Edmund to regain control of Scotland.

Duncan had lived the first twelve years of his life as King Malcolm's son in Scotland. He was detained as a hostage in England for fifteen years, was free for seven years, and then was king in Scotland briefly. In this biography, he was similar to Edward the Exile.

Edmund (aged about twenty-two) and Donald (aged about sixty) were able to come to terms on a partnership. They would attempt to divide Scotland, putting Edmund in control of the southern part. Control of the country was now more evenly divided than it had been before Duncan's intrusion.

In England, William II was frustrated again. Obviously, he felt that Edmund was another troublemaker like his father, Malcolm, had been with his raids into Northumberland. The Gaelic-speaking Donald Ban was trying to undo the English language reform in Scotland that Margaret had begun. It would be much more profitable for business to promote Scotland's changeover to the English language.

William II needed a military leader who was familiar with Scotland and who had some useful contacts with the people there. Who could be better than Edgar Aethling? Edgar knew Scotland and had friends there. Plus, Malcolm and Margaret still had several sons available who knew Edgar.

In 1097, William II provided a force of about two hundred knights to Edgar. They slipped into Scotland and soon gathered a large group of supporters. In November, this force surprised Donald and Edmund, and thus were able to overthrow the two kings of Scotland. To complete the coup, Edgar installed not himself, but his nephew and his namesake Edgar, to the Scottish throne.[106] Success! At the age of about forty-six, Edgar had finally achieved something noteworthy.

To dispose of the former leaders, Donald was tortured and lost his eyesight in the process. Edmund was sent to a monastery. Both of these men died just a few years later (c. 1100), which made Donald about sixty-seven years old at his death. But Edmund was only about twenty-eight years old when he died, thus making the cause of his death yet another mystery.

Beginning with their son Edgar in 1097, the descendants of Malcolm and Margaret reigned over Scotland for almost the next two hundred years. Historians praised Margaret for the virtuous education that she provided her children, thus giving her credit for this lengthy time of stability. The nation was almost always at peace.

The First Crusade

In 1096, Pope Urban II[107] issued a call to arms, seeking a crusade to retake the Holy Land. As much of Europe was now united in this new cause, Edgar responded. Finished in Scotland in November of 1097, Edgar immediately took command of a fleet of ships and set sail with his knights from Scotland and England to the far end of the Mediterranean Sea. Before the end of March 1098, the fleet had reached Antioch[108] (modern-day Hatay) in present-day Turkey. Edgar had his men burn their ships, which had become worn by the long trip, for firewood. He then joined the other Crusade forces on land. Once again, Edgar was reunited with his old friend Robert Curthose, who commanded a large Norman army. Robert had worked out a deal with William II to mortgage his land in Normandy as means to help finance the crusade.

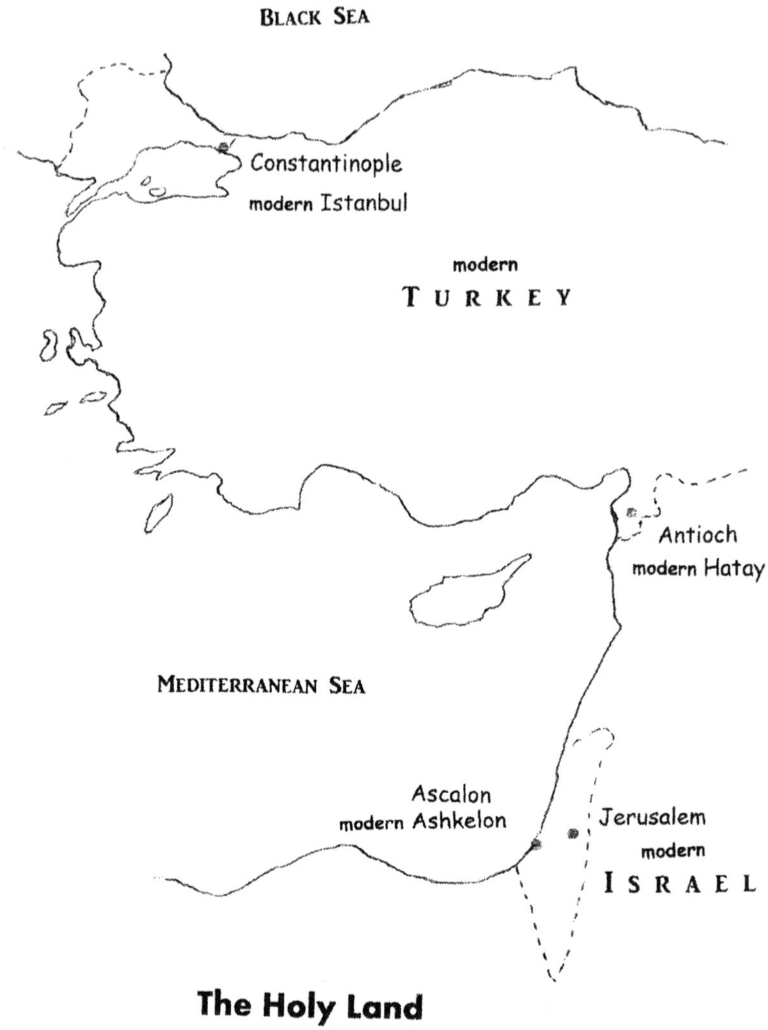

The Holy Land

Edgar's forces had arrived at Antioch at a crucial time. The Crusaders had laid siege to Antioch starting the previous October. As Edgar's forces and more reinforcements coming from Europe arrived, the Crusaders were able to increase pressure on the city. Robert Curthose fought heroically and led his forces to a significant victory during the siege. It would be June before the city fell. Once Antioch was secure, the Crusaders were able to advance by land to Jerusalem. It took the large army most of a year to do this.[109] Upon sighting the holy city, Edgar took part in a religious delirium that cannot be imagined in modern times; the Crusaders embraced one another, wept, and kissed the ground.

Another leader of the Crusade whom Edgar would likely have known was an itinerant preacher named Peter the Hermit.[110] Peter had led the first crusade army to leave Europe, a poorly organized force that had even included women and children. Peter had a near fanatical faith, but much of his army had been lost or dispersed by the time they left Antioch. Edgar may have found Peter to be a charismatic leader, but he would have been severely disappointed by the latter's impractical leadership skills.

Still, Peter found a way to lead the army at Jerusalem. Undoubtedly inspired by the biblical description of Joshua leading the Israelites to their miraculous capture of the city of Jericho, Peter led the Crusaders by marching barefoot in a religious procession around the walls of the city once each day for six consecutive days. Then the Crusaders attacked.

Once the Crusaders broke through the walls of Jerusalem, the fighting turned into a massacre that lasted for seven days. The Crusaders' conquest of Jerusalem was complete in July of 1099.

In Jerusalem, a certain resident is said to have shown the Crusaders a piece of wood that, he said, had come from the True Cross. This man claimed that this priceless object had been passed down through many generations and also had been kept a secret from the Muslims. This stirred up more rejoicing among the Crusaders. So now Edgar was able to see and touch another part of the True Cross, a different portion of which his sister Margaret possessed in Scotland. But once again, the authenticity of this artifact is open to question.

The First Crusade had achieved its primary objective, but another threat arose when a large Egyptian army appeared to the southwest of Jerusalem. Robert Curthose was one of the leaders who led the Crusaders to meet the enemy. They made sure to take the newfound piece of the True Cross with them. On August 12, 1099, the Crusaders attacked at Ascalon (modern-day Ashkelon)[111] and forced the Egyptians to retreat. This was the final battle in the First Crusade, with the Crusaders in complete control of the Holy Land.[112]

William of Malmesbury records the heroism and martyrdom of a close friend of Edgar's named Robert Godwin:

> [The Crusaders] rushed through the midst of the enemy, by the assistance of Robert alone, who ... hewed down the Turks, on either hand, with his drawn sword; but, while excited to greater ferocity by his success, he was pressing on with too much eagerness, his sword dropped from his hand, and when stooping down to recover it, he was surrounded by a multitude, and cast into chains. Taken thence to Babylon, as they report, when he refused to deny Christ, he was placed as a mark in the middle of the market-place, and being transfixed with darts, died a martyr.[113]

The loss of this friend caused Edgar some considerable grief, but Godwin's death as a martyr would have reinforced Edgar's Christian convictions.

Robert Curthose hurried back to Normandy in 1100, whereas Edgar returned home more slowly. The two friends had worked and fought alongside Crusaders from countries all across Europe, thus building many strong relationships with the leaders of those countries. By the time Edgar determined to return to England, he had gained great respect among the Crusade army. This was the greatest success that Edgar ever experienced. And his success was recognized.

Edgar likely traveled to Constantinople (modern-day Istanbul), the capital of the Byzantine Empire,[114] which governed much of what we recognize as Turkey and Greece, and was ruled by Alexius I.[115] Edgar was given a rich gift for his service in the Crusade. He also received an offer of a position in the empire, which he declined.

In Constantinople, Edgar would have seen and touched the most amazing of all Christian artifacts, the burial shroud of Christ, which is now known as the Shroud of Turin, as it is now kept in Turin, Italy. The shroud was known to be in Constantinople at this time. As a special guest of Alexius, Edgar certainly would have been given an opportunity to see it.[116]

He would have been fortunate as well, for the shroud was certainly in better condition at that time, before being fire-damaged as it is now.

Constantinople at that time was the center of the Eastern Orthodox churches, as the split between the Eastern Church and the Roman Catholic Church had occurred in 1054. Edgar likely would have learned about the differences between these two churches that caused this split.

Farther on the way to England, Edgar stopped in Germany, which was being ruled by Henry IV[117] of the Salian Dynasty, who was in a struggle to remain in power. Here Edgar was also given a rich gift for his service to the Crusade and received an offer of a position in the government. But Edgar declined this offer, as he was determined to return home. There had been another change to the throne of England. Edgar and his friend Robert Curthose believed that they had another opportunity. William of Malmesbury commented, "Edgar … gave up everything, through regard to his native soil. For, truly, the love of their country deceives some men to such a degree, that nothing seems pleasant to them, unless they can breathe their native air. Edgar, therefore, deluded by this silly desire, returned to England."[118] Obviously, William of Malmesbury believed that Edgar was mistaken or foolish to have declined these choice job offers and to embroil himself in the English monarchy again.

One More Rebellion

August 2nd, 1100. ***"I, Walter Tirel, had the honor of hunting with King William II of England. William was looking for game, whereas I had a more important and profitable target in my sight. This is how it happened: the time was about an hour or so before sunset when William's arrow found a stag. I complimented William on his good aim. The wounded animal had yet to fall and began moving to our left. As we watched, William placed his hand to his forehead to shield his eyes from the sun. My opportunity was now! I quickly turned. From a distance of no more than five paces, my arrow flew true and deep into William's chest. I shall not forget the look from his eyes toward me, even though it was only a momentary glance. A very tough man was William; he even managed to break the end of arrow before he landed on the ground. I quickly reached Henry, William's brother, and received***

my payment. I even had darkness to cover my getaway. I have no further use of England; I shall be prospering in France. Henry will grant a pardon on my behalf! They will even concoct a story that this was an accident! You have to understand Henry's view; he was ready to be the king, and he needed to strike before Robert Curthose returned from the Crusade. For Henry and me, this had been a most profitable day."

Henry, the youngest of the sons of William the Conqueror, was in fact very nearby when William died. He immediately seized the throne, thus becoming Henry I. Although there is a story alleging that William's death was an accident, the timing of this event plus Henry being close by lends strong support to the case that this was an assassination. In any event, there is debate over this matter.[119]

Coming from the Crusade, Robert Curthose was able to reach Normandy in September, only to discover that once again he had been bypassed for the throne. Robert quickly began to gather support for himself, as he was once again forming a rebellion, this one against yet another brother. Henry I attempted to prevent any fighting by meeting with Robert and promising to pay him for his loyalty. For a while, the two were reconciled. But then it became obvious that Henry was, just as William II had done before him, not going to honor his part of the agreement. Robert then began an armed rebellion. When Edgar returned from the Crusade, he once again took up the role of an adviser for the cause of his friend. Perhaps Edgar still thought that he might have one more chance to regain the throne of England. But there was very little fighting as the brothers continued to negotiate their differences.

In 1106, fighting did break out, but the rebellion was concluded with a battle at Tinchebray,[120] in Normandy. Edgar and Robert were captured by the forces under Henry I. To be taken as a prisoner of war has to be the one of the most shocking and humiliating of all things to happen to a soldier. This was especially true for Edgar and Robert since they were war heroes of the Crusade. For Edgar, this was yet another deep disappointment.

Edgar and Robert were taken to face Henry I. Edgar did find some luck here, as his niece Edith (she had taken the name Matilda when she married), the daughter of Margaret and Malcolm, had married

Henry I in 1100. With a favorable family connection, Edgar was granted a pardon and then was released, although probably to endure house arrest. Robert Curthose was imprisoned for the remainder of his life, although this was considered to be house arrest. About Robert's imprisonment and character: Robert "was provided with abundance both of amusement and of food. He was confined, however, till he had survived all his companions in the Crusade, nor was he liberated to the day of his death. He was so eloquent in his native tongue, that none could be more pleasant; in other men's affairs, no counselor was more excellent; in military skill equal to any; yet, through the easiness of his disposition, was he ever esteemed unfit to have the management of the state."[121]

There was no further conflict for who would hold the English throne during Edgar's lifetime. King Henry I reigned securely until his death in 1135. Best of all, with the influence of Matilda's being married to the English monarch, the two nations Scotland and England began to enjoy many years of relative peace and security.

Edgar's Last Days

William of Malmesbury recorded only that Edgar was believed to have returned to Scotland in about 1120. Later, Malmesbury confirmed that Edgar was still living in 1125. He writes of Edgar, "After various revolutions of fortune, he now grows old in the country in privacy and quiet."[122] The teenage boy Edgar who had been labeled as the "child Edgar" was now gracefully growing old. He had found peace at last.

After that, I can find nothing more to record about Edgar's life. He vanished into the mists of history. The final entry for Edgar's life, placed just because the historian and the biographer needed something to end with, reads that Edgar was "thought to have been in Scotland, and thought to have died around 1126." For Edgar, there are no remains, no gravesite, and no memorial.

So what do we make of Edgar's life? As a young child, he knew the tragedy of losing his father. As a teenager, he was elevated to king before being forced to abdicate. He rebelled and left England, at which time he fought losing battles. He was shipwrecked in a storm at sea and was nearly lost. As a young man, he became known as "Edgar the Outlaw," terrorizing northern England. As a middle-aged man, he fought against the Normans in England for at least ten years—and he lost. As an older man, he became a prisoner of war.

Edgar enjoyed two successes: overturning the king of Scotland to restore his nephew to the throne, and the First Crusade. His successes occurred between 1097 and 1102.

There is one more aspect of Edgar's life to mention. Let him tell us: ***"I am a man of my word. I promised and I vowed that I should never marry or have children unless I was in my rightful place on the throne of England. I have missed some joy and excitement, certainly, that most people end up taking for granted. You see, God had another purpose for my life. My family, the House of Wessex, had failed long ago, long before my birth. The Almighty knew that the House of Wessex would end with me. I know now, after my life of striving, that His ways are not the ways that a person would choose. Only now, past 70 years of age, do I see God's plan for my life. I shall give praise to the Lord."***

But what Edgar knew and experienced makes him one of the amazing characters of all history. Consider the following things: He lived as royalty, but he also slept overnight on battlefields. He had the best education of the time (the eleventh century), but he spent much of his life with knights. He experienced the royal life, the common life, and the life of house arrest. He survived disasters and battles.

What a wealth of knowledge of languages Edgar must have had! He knew English and, as a young child, learned an Eastern European/Hungarian language. He would have learned French in Normandy, probably some Italian, and probably Latin for church. Maybe he would have learned even more languages.

He traveled from Scotland to the Holy Land, and many places in between, covering much of the known world at that time. And when he traveled, he lived in those lands. In that time, there was no dropping in somewhere and then flying away a few hours later. He really got to know the geography, the weather, the people, and the plant and animal life where he went.

Edgar knew how to govern a country as a king. He also knew what decisions a king had the power to make. He could see what would be politically popular or possible, and what wouldn't succeed. As a general, he had learned to direct a battle strategically and tactically. He knew what his knights on horseback could do, and he saw how the foot soldiers and the archers fought. He knew what it was like to sail over a long distance through all types of weather. He could direct the siege of a castle or defend a castle. Including conditions from the cold of the winter in Scotland to the heat of the summer in the Holy Land, he experienced every type of combat for that time period.

Through all of this, Edgar, I am convinced, was dedicated to the cause of the church and to Christ. He was raised in a family that honored Christ in many ways and often through day and night. His sisters Margaret and Christina likely influenced him as an adult to stay firmly committed to the church. Edgar would have seen the True Cross that Margaret possessed. The Crusade to Jerusalem was another occasion during which he would have regarded the importance of religion. Seeing the amazing burial shroud of Christ in Constantinople would have provided confirmation of his faith.

So now it is 1124 in Scotland. Edgar is approaching his mid-seventies. You, Edgar, look back on your life. In spite of all the battles you have experienced, you are now past the average life expectancy for your time period. Your fighting days are past. Tending a garden or doing carpentry is about all you can physically manage anymore. You have outlived both of your sisters, Margaret and Christina. In fact, you have outlived seven of your eight nephews and nieces, whose parents were Margaret and Malcolm. Your last remaining nephew, David, is reigning as king of Scotland and is at least kindly making sure that you have shelter and food. Do you get to see him? Do you offer him advice?

With most of your life past, what do you think about? Do you regret the lost opportunities, or can you still look forward? Are you sorry that you never married or had children? Is your sorrow such that you try to cover your pain with drink, or are you still finding a small way to contribute to the church and enjoying the company of the last few friends you have left? Or are you doing all of these things?

If the congregation of the church that is now the Borthwick Parish Church began to meet in 1124, and if some of your last friends are involved in building it, wouldn't you at least contribute to the building? Even if the church is only a little more than a temporary shelter at this point, wouldn't you take the ride out from Edinburgh to visit the church on the occasion of the congregants' first Christmas there? What recollections could you offer when you got there? What would be your message?

Let's drop in and visit!

Endnotes

1 "Cerdic, King of the West Saxons," *Geni.com,* accessed March 2, 2015, http://www.geni.com/people/Cerdic-King-of-the-West-Saxons/6000000002142247689.

2 "Edgar the Peaceful," *English Monarchs,* accessed March 2, 2015, http://www.englishmonarchs.co.uk/saxon_12.htm.

3 "Ælfthryth, wife of Edgar," *Wikipedia,* accessed March 2, 2015, http://en.wikipedia.org/wiki/%C3%86lfthryth,_wife_of_Edgar.

4 Father Nektarios Serfes, "The Life of among the Saints Edward the Martyr, King of England," *Serfes.org,* accessed March 2, 2015, http://www.serfes.org/lives/stedward.htm.

5 Biography Base, *Edward the Martyr Biography,* accessed March 2, 2015 http://www.biographybase.com/biography/Edward_the_Martyr.html,

6 Biography Base, *Edward the Martyr Biography*

7 Biography Base, *Edward the Martyr Biography*

8 "Great Schism," accessed August 12, 2015, http://www.theopedia.com/Great-Schism,

9 *The Anglo-Saxon Chronicle,* year 978, *BritanniaHistory.com,* accessed March 2, 2015, http://www.britannia.com/history/docs/973-79.html.

10 Thomas Forester, trans., *The Chronicle of Florence of Worcester* (London: Henry G. Bohn, 1854), accessed March 2, 2015, http://books.google.com/books?id=gpR0iz5GjYgC&printsec=titlepage#v=onepage&q&f=true, 126.

11 "Edward the Martyr," *St. Nicholas Russian Orthodox Church,* accessed March 2, 2015, http://www.orthodox.net/western-saints/edward.html.

12 "Aethelred the Unready," *Geni.com,* accessed March 2, 2015, http://www.geni.com/people/%C3%86thelred-the-Unready-King-of-the-English/6000000000769899901.

13 "Emma of Normandy," *Wikipedia,* accessed March 2, 2015, http://en.wikipedia.org/wiki/Emma_of_Normandy.

14 "Swein Forkbeard," *Wikipedia,* accessed March 2, 2015, http://en.wikipedia.org/wiki/Sweyn_Forkbeard.

15 "Cnut the Great," *Wikipedia,* accessed Auguat 12, 2015, http://en.wikipedia.org/wiki/Cnut_the_Great.

16 "Edmund Ironside," *Wikipedia,* accessed August 12, 2015, http://en.wikipedia.org/wiki/Edmund_Ironside.

17 "Ealdgyth," *Wikipedia,* accessed August 12, 2015, http://en.wikipedia.org/wiki/Ealdgyth%28floruit_1015%E2%80%931016%29.

18 "The Battle of Assandun" (also called the Battle of Ashingdon), *Wikipedia,* accessed March 2, 2015, http://en.wikipedia.org/wiki/Battle_of_Assandun.

19 "Edward 'the Exile', Ætheling of England," *Geni.com,* accessed August 12, 2015, http://www.geni.com/people/Edward-the-Exile- %C3%86theling-of-England/6000000009432470359
20 "Ælfgifu of Northampton," *Yahoo.com,* accessed August 12, 2015, https://en.wikipedia.org/wiki/%C3%86lfgifu_of_Northampton
21 "Harold Harefoot," *Wikipedia,* accessed August 12, 2015, https://en.wikipedia.org/wiki/Harold_Harefoot
22 "Harthacnut," *Wikipedia,* accessed August 12, 2015, http://en.wikipedia.org/wiki/Harthacnut.
23 "Ingigerd Olofsdotter, of Sweden" *Wikipedia,* accessed August 12, 2015 http://en.wikipedia.org/wiki/Ingegerd_Olofsdotter_of_Sweden.
24 "Yaroslav the Wise," *Wikipedia,* accessed August 12, 2015, https://en.wikipedia.org/wiki/Yaroslav_the_Wise
25 "Stephen I of Hungary," *Wikipedia,* accessed August 12, 2015, http://en.wikipedia.org/wiki/Stephen_I_of_Hungary.
26 "Edward the Confessor," *Wikipedia,* accessed August 12, 2015, http://en.wikipedia.org/wiki/Edward_the_Confessor.
27 "Edith of Wessex," *Wikipedia,* accessed August 12, 2015, https://en.wikipedia.org/wiki/Edith_of_Wessex
28 "Godwin, Earl of Wessex," *Wikipedia,* accessed August 12, 2015, https://en.wikipedia.org/wiki/Godwin,_Earl_of_Wessex
29 "Harold Godwinson" (also known as Harold II), *Wikipedia,* accessed August 12, 2015, https://en.wikipedia.org/wiki/Harold_Godwinson
30 William the Conqueror", accessed March 2, 2015 http://en.wikipedia.org/wiki/William_the_Conqueror
31 "Peter Orseolo," *Wikipedia,* accessed August 12, 2015, http://en.wikipedia.org/wiki/Peter,_King_of_Hungary
32 "Agatha," *Wikipedia,* accessed August 12, 2015, http://en.wikipedia.org/wiki/Agatha,_wife_of_Edward_the_Exile
33 "Margaret," *Wikipedia,* accessed August 12, 2015, http://en.wikipedia.org/wiki/Saint_Margaret_of_Scotland Also see William Forbes-Leith Turgot, SJ, Bishop of St. Andrews, ed., *The Life of St. Margaret, Queen of Scotland,* 3rd edition (Edinburgh: David Douglas, 1896), http://mw.mcmaster.ca/scriptorium/margaret.html (accessed April 27, 2015). This book is a fascinating biography of Margaret.
34 "Christina," *Wikipedia,* accessed March 2, 2015, http://en.wikipedia.org/wiki/Cristina,_daughter_of_Edward_the_Exile
35 "Edgar the Æthling," *Wikipedia,* accessed August 12, 2015, https://en.wikipedia.org/wiki/Edgar_the_%C3%86theling
36 "Castle Reka," *Wikipedia,* accessed March 2, 2015, http://en.wikipedia.org/wiki/Castle_R%C3%A9ka

37 "Anastasia of Kiev" *Wikipedia*, accessed August 12, 2015, http://en.wikipedia.org/wiki/Anastasia_of_Kiev

38 "Andrew I of Hungary," *Wikipedia*, accessed March 2, 2015, http://en.wikipedia.org/wiki/Andrew_I_of_Hungary

39 "William the Seemly Sinclair," *Geni.com*, accessed April 13, 2015, http://www.geni.com/people/William-the-Seemly-Sinclair-of-Roslin/6000000002187978452

40 Lang Syne Publishers Ltd 2008, *Borthwick, The Origins Of The Clan Borthwick And Their Place In Scotland's History*, page 13 Andreas the Hungarian is named as ancestor in this booklet which describes highlights of the history of the Borthwick Clan in Scotland

41 Clifford Stanley Sims, "Leslie (Walter de Leslin)," *The Origin and Significance of Scottish Surnames* (New York: Avenal Books, 1964), 67. This book provides a brief background of many Scottish names, including the names of the families the Leslies, the Livingstones, the Sinclairs, and the Borthwicks.

42 Sims, "Livingstone (Livingus)," in *Scottish Surnames*, 69.

43 Sims, "Leslie (Barthlomew)," in *Scottish Surnames*, 67.

44 "Edward the Exile," *Geni.com*, accessed March 2, 2015, http://www.geni.com/people/Edward-the-Exile-%C3%86theling-of- England/6000000009432470359. On various we sites there is much uncertainty as to exactly when this happened in the years 1056-7.

45 "Harold II" (also known as Harold Godwinson), *Encyclopædia Britannica*, accessed March 2, 2015, http://www.britannica.com/EBchecked/topic/255667/Harold-II

46 *The Anglo-Saxon Chronicle*, year 1057, *Britannia History.com*, accessed March 2, 2015, http://www.britannia.com/history/docs/1056-63.html

47 "Matilda of Flanders," *Wikipedia*, accessed August 12, 2015, http://en.wikipedia.org/wiki/Matilda_of_Flanders

48 "Robert Curthose," *Wikipedia*, accessed March 2, 2015, http://en.wikipedia.org/wiki/Robert_Curthose

49 "William II of England" (also known as William Rufus), *Wikipedia*, accessed March 2, 2015, http://en.wikipedia.org/wiki/William_II_of_England

50 "Henry I of England," *Wikipedia*, accessed August 12, 2015, http://en.wikipedia.org/wiki/Henry_I_of_England

51 "Malcolm III of Scotland" *Wikipedia*, accessed March 2, 2015, http://en.wikipedia.org/wiki/Malcolm_III_of_Scotland See also Stewart Ross, "Malcolm III," in *Monarchs of Scotland* (New York: Facts on File, 1990) 42–45.

52 "Lulach," *Wikipedia, accessed* March 2, 2015, http://en.wikipedia.org/wiki/Lulach See also Ross, "Lulach," in *Monarchs of Scotland*, 41.

53 "Macbeth, King of Scotland," *Wikipedia,* accessed March 2, 2015, http://en.wikipedia.org/wiki/Macbeth,_King_of_Scotland See also Ross, "Macbeth," in *Monarchs of Scotland,* 39.

54 "Ingibjorg Finnsdottir," *Geni.com,* accessed August 12, 2015, https://en.wikipedia.org/wiki/Ingibiorg_Finnsdottir

55 "Duncan II of Scotland," *Wikipedia,* accessed August 12, 2015, http://en.wikipedia.org/wiki/Duncan_II_of_Scotland. See also Ross, *Monarchs of Scotland,* 46–48.

56 *The Anglo-Saxon Chronicle,* year 1066, *BritanniaHistory.com,* accessed March 2, 2015 http://www.britannia.com/history/docs/1066.html.

57 "Harald Hardrada," *Wikipedia,* accessed August 12, 2015, http://en.wikipedia.org/wiki/Harald_Hardrada.

58 "Tostig Godwinson," *Wikipedia,* accessed August 12, 2015, https://en.wikipedia.org/wiki/Tostig_Godwinson

59 "Battle of Stamford Bridge," *Wikipedia,* accessed August 12, 2015, https://en.wikipedia.org/wiki/Battle_of_Stamford_Bridge

60 "The Battle of Hastings," accessed March 2, 2015, http://en.wikipedia.org/wiki/Battle_of_Hastings.

61 "The Tapestry Kit Collection," *The Bayeux Tapestry: A Guide,* accessed March 2, 2015, http://www.bayeux-tapestry.org.uk/.

62 "Berkhampstead Castle," *Wikipedia,* accessed August 12, 2015, http://en.wikipedia.org/wiki/Berkhamsted_Castle

63 *The Anglo-Saxon Chronicle,* year 1066, *BritanniaHistory.com,* http://www.britannia.com/history/docs/1066.html.

64 *The Anglo-Saxon Chronicle,* year 1067, *BritanniaHistory.com,* http://www.britannia.com/history/docs/1067-69.html.

65 *The Anglo-Saxon Chronicle,* year 1067

66 Swyrich Corporation, "Boyes Family Crest, Coat of Arms and Name History," *House of Names,* accessed June 2, 2015, https://www.houseofnames.com/boyes-family-crest. This identical phrase, "Granted lands by Duke William of Normandy, their liege Lord, for their distinguished assistance at the battle of Hastings in 1066 A.D.," is repeated to describe many of these clans on different websites. The names of Scottish clans that I have found where the clan was founded after the Norman invasion include Allan, Boyes/Bois/Boyce, Brooks, Burnett, Elliot, Frazer, Fitzstephen/Stephen, Goodall, Jardine, Kirk, Lyle, Lyon, Maule, Morton, Paul, Rollo, Somerville, Stewart, and Trail.

67 *The Anglo-Saxon Chronicle,* year 1068, *BritanniaHistory.com,* accessed August 12, 2015, http://www.britannia.com/history/docs/1067-69.html.

68 "Sweyn II of Denmark," *Wikipedia,* accessed August 12, 2015, http://en.wikipedia.org/wiki/Sweyn_II_of_Denmark

69 *The Anglo-Saxon Chronicle,* year 1069, *BritanniaHistory.com,* http://www.britannia.com/history/docs/1067-.html. Also see "York," *Wikipedia,* accessed August 12, 2015, http://en.wikipedia.org/wiki/York

70 From Books LLC, *History of Scotland by Period: Early Modern Scotland, Medieval Scotland, Prehistoric Scotland, Dal Riata, Edgar the ?theling,* (Memphis, Tennessee, 2010), page 179

71 Brittania History.com, *The Anglo-Saxon Chronicle,* Year 1069

72 Books LLC, *History of Scotland by Period:* page 179

73 Brittania History.com, *The Anglo-Saxon Chronicle,* Year 1074

74 Brittania History.com, *The Anglo-Saxon Chronicle,* Year 1074

75 Brittania History.com, *The Anglo-Saxon Chronicle,* year 1068

76 Ross, "Edmund," in *Monarchs of Scotland,* page 48

77 Ross, "Edgar," in *Monarchs of Scotland,* page 49.

78 Ross, "Alexander," in *Monarchs of Scotland,* pages 50–52.

79 "Matilda of Scotland," *Wikipedia,* accessed August 12, 2015, https://en.wikipedia.org/wiki/Matilda_of_Scotland

80 "MaryofScotland, CountessofBoulogne," *Wikipedia,* accessed August 12, 2015, http://en.wikipedia.org/wiki/Mary_of_Scotland,_Countess_of_Boulogne

81 Ross, "David" in *Monarchs Of Scotland,* pages 52-55

82 Turgot, *The Life of St. Margaret,* chapter 1, paragraph 7.

83 "Dunfermline Abbey," *Wikipedia,* accessed August 12, 2015, http://en.wikipedia.org/wiki/Dunfermline_Abbey

84 "St. Margaret's Stone," *ScottishChurches.org,* accessed August 12, 2015, http://www.scottishchurches.org.uk/sites/site/id/10428/name/St+Margaret%27s+Stone+Dunfermline+Fife

85 "St. Margaret's Cave," Fife Direct, accessed August 12, 2015, http://www.fifedirect.org.uk/atoz/index.cfm? fuseaction=facility.display&facid=8F8C0CF3-22B0-4F4B-A390CD687136B1C6

86 "Holyrood (Cross)," *Wiki 2,* accessed August 12, 2015, https://en.wiki2.org/wiki/Holyrood_%28cross%29

87 Turgot, *The Life of St. Margaret,* end note 43.

88 "Ell Conversion," *UnitConversion.org,* accessed March 2, 2015, http://www.unitconversion.org/length/ell-conversion.html

89 Books LLC, *History of Scotland,* 179.

90 "Norman Conquest of Southern Italy," *Wikipedia,* accessed August 12, 2015, http://en.wikipedia.org/wiki/Norman_conquest_of_southern_Italy

91 Books LLC, *History of Scotland,* 180.

92 Books LLC, *History of Scotland,* 180

93 Turgot, *The Life of St. Margaret,* chapter III, paragraph 23.

94 William T. Jarvis, "Fasting," *NCAHF,* accessed March 24, 2015, http://www.ncahf.org/articles/e-i/fasting.html

95 Turgot, *The Life of St. Margaret,* chapter IV, paragraphs 33–34.

96 Turgot, *The Life of St. Margaret,* chapter IV, paragraphs 33–34.

97 Turgot, *The Life of St. Margaret,* chapter IV, paragraph 37.

98 "Battle of Alnwick (1093)," *Wikipedia,* accessed August 12, 2015, http://en.wikipedia.org/wiki/Battle_of_Alnwick_%281093%29

99 Ross, "Edgar," in *Monarchs of Scotland,* page 49.

100 Turgot, *The Life of St. Margaret,* Chapter IV, paragraph 40

101 Turgot, *The Life of St. Margaret,* Chapter IV, paragraph 40

102 Turgot, *The Life of St. Margaret,* Chapter IV, paragraph 41

103 St Margaret's Chapel, Edinburgh, *Wikipedia,* accessed August 12, 2015, http://en.wikipedia.org/w/index.php?title=St_Margaret%27s_Chapel,_Edinburgh&oldid=637940534

104 "Donald III of Scotland," *Wikipedia,* accessed August 12, 2015, http://en.wikipedia.org/w/index.php?title=Donald_III_of_Scotland&oldid=641314120

105 "Duncan II of Scotland," *Wikipedia,* accessed August 12, 2015, http://en.wikipedia.org/w/index.php?title=Duncan_II_of_Scotland&oldid=639173463

106 Ross, "Edgar," in *Monarchs of Scotland,* page 49.

107 "Pope Urban II," *Wikipedia,* accessed August 12, 2015, http://en.wikipedia.org/w/index.php?title=Pope_Urban_II&oldid=645087193.

108 "Antakya," *Wikipedia,* accessed August 12, 2015, http://en.wikipedia.org/w/index.php?title=Antakya&oldid=645201194

109 "Jerusalem," *Wikipedia,* accessed August 12, 2015, http://en.wikipedia.org/w/index.php?title=Jerusalem&oldid=647653351

110 "Peter the Hermit," *Wikipedia,* accessed August 12, 2015, http://en.wikipedia.org/w/index.php?title=Peter_the_Hermit&oldid=636007299

111 "Ascalon," *Wikipedia,* accessed August 12, 2015, http://en.wikipedia.org/w/index.php?title=Ascalon&oldid=646737132

112 "First Crusade," *Wikipedia,* accessed August 12, 2015, http://en.wikipedia.org/w/index.php?title=First_Crusade&oldid=647843018

113 Internet Archive, "William of Malmesbury's *Chronicle of the Kings of England, from the Earliest Period to the Reign of King Stephen,*" accessed March 2, 2015, http://archive.org/stream/williamofmalmesb1847will/williamofmalmesb1847will_djvu.txt, 284.

114 "Byzantine Empire," *Wikipedia,* accessed August 12, 2015, http://en.wikipedia.org/w/index.php?title=Byzantine_Empire&oldid=647630163

115 "Alexios I Komnenos," *Wikipedia,* accessed August 12, 2015, http://en.wikipedia.org/w/index.php?title=Alexios_I_Komnenos&oldid=642352479

116 Dr. John Jackson, "Noted Accomplishments of TSC," *Turin Shroud Center of Colorado,* accessed February 19, 2015, http://www.shroudofturin.com/

accomplishments2.html See also Ian Wilson, "Chronology of the Turin Shroud," in *The Blood and the Shroud* (New York: The Free Press, 1998), 268–273, which indicates that the shroud was brought into Constantinople on August 15, 944, and was removed when the city was sacked early in 1204.

117 "Henry IV, Holy Roman Emperor," *Wikipedia,* accessed August 12, 2015, http://en.wikipedia.org/w/index.php?title=Henry_IV,_Holy_Roman_Emperor&oldid=644532944

118 Internet Archive, "William of Malmesbury's *Chronicle of the Kings of England,*" 284–5.

119 "William II of England," *Wikipedia for Schools,* accessed August 12, 2015, http://schools-wikipedia.org/wp/w/William_II_of_England.htm (A lengthy article provided on this page debates whether William II died by accident or by assassination.)

120 "Battle of Tinchebray," *Wikipedia,* accessed August 12, 2015, http://en.wikipedia.org/w/index.php?title=Battle_of_Tinchebray&oldid=635644745

121 Internet Archive, "William of Malmesbury's *Chronicle of the Kings of England,*" 423.

122 Internet Archive, "William of Malmesbury's *Chronicle of the Kings of England,*" 253.

Edgar Reminisces

This will be the scene: The church is one simple room, but even that has been just partly completed. One door is at the center of one of the long walls. A fireplace dominates the wall opposite, which is long. The fireplace is at the center of the stone wall, and the new stone glistens nicely. The other walls and roof are made of wood and thatch, so they are rather dark. There is another door to the right of the fireplace. The fireplace is quite long, and there is a nice fire going. Several pots of food are being warmed. Some fish are also being prepared, and several strips of smoked venison are laid out. The first Christmas in the church is to be celebrated with a meal for the entire extended family. It is a good to have the fireplace going, because outside the weather includes some light rain and a very cool breeze. Inside the church walls, it is rather cool, but when the people gather, it is cozy and warm—and the food gives pleasant aromas.

These will be our characters(fictional) that we will place around Edgar: Constance is the oldest member of the family and is the only one remaining who came from Hungary. Her health is not very good, as she is almost eighty years old. The other family members that appear in this fictional account are Constance's son Andrus; his wife, Martha; and their children: John, who is about eighteen years old and who is beginning to study for the priesthood; Andrew, who is about eleven years old; and Margie, who is about eight years old. Constance's other son is William. William's wife is Agnes, and their children are Edward, about nine, and Edith, about seven. Both Andrus and William fought in the Crusade under Edgar's command. Their descendants will become the Borthwicks, but the name Borthwick has not yet been created.

Edgar Aetheling's carriage driver is Roadie. Tat is the name of the house cat. Edgar, of course, is our man that we want to listen to and learn from. Both of these families live nearby to the new church.

The Gathering at the Church

Martha, Agnes, Margie, and Edith were cooking and cleaning inside the church. Tat the house cat is asleep beneath the table.

Martha said, "Margie, Edith, I want you to go outside to get a branch to decorate."

Margie replied, "Mother, it's very cold outside."

Martha said, "Find something quickly, then."

The two girls hurried out the door.

Agnes was close to the fireplace. Martha asked her, "Will there be enough food for everyone?"

Agnes replied, "I think there will be enough, but I don't know who is going to come with King Edgar. Will he bring a whole army with him?"

Martha said, "Of course he is not going to do that. Indeed, Andrus said that Edgar will have only a driver with him."

Agnes asked, "Can he do that as man who was king?"

Martha replied, "That was a long time ago when he was king, so he is almost by himself. I suppose you could say that he is no longer important enough to have a group around him."

Andrus, William, John, Andrew, and Edward entered the room. Andrus asked, "Is our meal getting ready? I can see a horse and carriage coming, so Edgar will be here soon."

Agnes said, "So just one horse and carriage? He does not have an army with him. That's good. We will have enough food for today. I hope there will be food for tomorrow."

William said, "Tomorrow we can find more food. And tomorrow we will start the day in prayer, asking God to provide. Tomorrow is another day that God will take care of."

The two girls, Edith and Margie, returned, each carrying a small sprig of an evergreen branch. Margie said, "We brought these, Mother."

Martha took the two sprigs and placed one on each side of the fireplace. She exclaimed, "That looks wonderful. We have a decoration for Christmas."

Andrus asked, "A decoration for Christmas? What can women think of next?"

William said, "I can't understand these women!" He shook his head. "I can hear the horse and carriage now. Edgar is just about here. I am looking forward to seeing Edgar and talking about old times."

Edward asked, "It's really King Edgar? The king of England?"

Andrew and Edward tried to hold some laughter to themselves. William noticed. "You boys will show the greatest respect to Edgar, as he is our guest. He was the king of England and I fought with him in the Crusade, so all of you children will listen attentively to him."

One of the adults opened the door near the fireplace to greet the guests. John quietly addressed the children, saying, "I know Edgar seems kind of old and crazy, but we have to listen to him."

Andrew asked, "He was here last summer, right?"

John replied, "Yes, that was him when we started building the church. But I think that he had been drinking when he was here."

The Entrance of Edgar

With the adults grouped near the door, Roadie led Edgar into the church. Edgar's face and clothes were wet, and his mostly white hair was matted strangely. Some of his ponytail was wrapped around his beard. All of the adults individually said "hello" or "welcome" to Edgar, but Edgar's discomfort was obvious. The children looked on, bemused.

Andrus asked, "What happened?"

Edgar replied, "Roadie determined to steer the horse into a tree branch, and when the branch turned there was water and ice and snow thrown all over me." Some of the adults laughed lightly. Roadie picked a dry napkin from the table and asked, "May I use this?" Martha nodded her consent.

Edgar said, "This is my driver, Roadie. I call him Roadie because when I need to travel, I can always count on him to take me down the road."

Roadie, after saying, "Sir, I am going to straighten you up," began to dry Edgar's face and put his hair back into place.

Edgar protested. "I am all right," he said.

But Roadie persisted. "Sir, your appearance is frightening to the little children. And I did not steer the horse into the tree branch. There, now that is better." Roadie said this last bit as he finished wiping Edgar's face. And now that Roadie was finished, Edgar did indeed look very distinguished, even with the short ponytail at the back of his hair.

Now comfortable, Edgar greeted all the adults by name. "Now that I can see, hello, Martha, Agnes. Andrus, so good to see you." He grasped Andrus's arm. He also had a sturdy handshake for William. "It's good to see you well." Edgar waved at several others in the back of the church and said, "This is a small shelter now, but it looks to be a fine start for the new church."

Andrus replied to Edgar, saying, "Sir, do you remember last summer when you here? We had just started putting the stone in around the base of the fireplace. There was nothing else in here at that time."

Edgar looked around. "Yes, I do remember. You have still got some more work to do, but today it looks very good." Then he looked at John. "Hello, John. I hear that you studying for the priesthood, young man."

John replied, "Yes, sir. I'm just starting, but I am sure that I can manage."

Edgar said, "Great, John. That is the highest calling." Then Edgar looked at the four children. "Well, look at this bunch. Tell me your names again."

Martha introduced each by name. "Edward and Edith are with Andrus and me. Andrew and Margie go with William and Agnes."

Edgar replied, "What a fine-looking group of lads and lasses. I do not remember you very well, for you have all changed so much." Looking at Edward, Edgar said, "Young man, I think you were about as tall as a baby sheep the last time I saw you."

Edward tried to smile. He replied, "I do remember you, sir."

Edgar said, "So, all of you, are your fathers teaching you well? And what I mean is that you must all learn how many trees in a row make six trees, or, if you like, how many eggs there are in six eggs." He looked to Edward.

Edward seemed puzzled by the simplicity of the question. He paused before he counted: "One, two, three, four, five, six. There are six trees in a row. There are six eggs. That's plain."

Edgar said, "Very well. In this world, you had better know how many trees in a row make six, because six trees may mark your property someday. And if you pay for six eggs, you had better have six eggs."

The Holyrood

Roadie had stepped outside. He now came back inside, carrying a black suitcase in the shape of a cross. He said to Edgar, "Edgar, here is the cross to show."

John asked, "Is this the Holyrood that I have heard about?"

Edgar replied, "Yes, it is the Holyrood. This is a day for us to celebrate, so I want everyone to see it." Roadie handed the case to Edgar. Edgar opened it, revealing a gold cross adorned with several precious stones, an ivory crucifix, and a small piece of wood at the center. As Edgar held the case with the cross inside, everyone took turns looking at it. "This is the Holyrood that my sister Margaret employed skilled craftsmen to make. Now, the length of wood in the center has come from the very cross upon which Christ was crucified. This is why I have brought it today, so that everyone in this church can see it and touch it."

William commented, "I have seen the cross before, but that was many years ago." Everyone was excited. John and the children were quite impressed as each touched the piece of wood.

Edgar then placed the cross inside the case. Putting the case on top of the fireplace mantle, he said, "I will set it here for today, but I will have to take it back with me when I leave. But today we will have it, as this is the first Christmas for the new church." As Edgar turned from the fireplace, he became worried. "Where is Constance? Is she all right?"

William answered, "She is still in the cabin. She has good days and not-so-good days."

Edgar immediately gave an order: "Bring her here! I want to see her."

William said, "I will see if we can get her up." He then left the room, taking Agnes with him.

Martha urged Edgar and Roadie to be seated. The two men sat down. John asked Edgar, "Where is the Holyrood kept?"

Edgar replied, "Now it is kept in the castle in Edinburgh. And it is not being used very often, so we have borrowed it for today. However, if the castle-keeper finds out that we have it, he might be very angry, so we need to keep this quiet." Edgar put his finger close to his mouth to indicate silence.

John asked, "So the Holyrood is very valuable?"

Edgar replied, "Oh yes, John. These gemstones by themselves are worth very much."

Roadie said to Edgar, "Sir, perhaps we should have brought an extra guard."

Edgar replied, "Silence, Roadie. Silence." He again held his finger up to indicate silence.

Roadie said, "Sir, the next time we take the Holyrood out, I will secure another guard."

John asked Edgar, "How many years have you had the Holyrood?"

Edgar replied, "Well, I have not had it in my possession. But, almost as far back as I can remember, my oldest sister, Margaret, the queen, had made it her special possession. She has been gone for quite a while now. Andrus, you and Martha met Queen Margaret, didn't you?"

Martha replied, "I do know of seeing her one time, but I was young, so I don't remember her very well."

Andrus answered, "I remember seeing her too. She spoke to me once. Very easy to like, she was."

Edgar said, "Everyone who ever met Margaret remembers her. As for me, she was my oldest sister—and no man should ever have an older sister. Her personality was a powerful force. Even when she was young, Margaret had some gems and the gold adornment added to the Holyrood so that she would like it better. That happened even before we came to Scotland. By the time we got to Scotland, the piece was famous."

John asked, "Did Margaret use the Holyrood as part of her missionary efforts?"

Edgar replied, "Yes, she did, some, but mostly she kept it close to herself. She used it for her own devotions. Now, when Margaret was queen and Malcolm was king, they would often take the Holyrood with them when they traveled. There would always be a group of soldiers protecting them and the Holyrood wherever they went. I traveled with them on a few occasions. Margaret was always looking for ways to show the faith to all of the various people whom she met. So when she did show the Holyrood, it became marvelous to behold for everyone we met. The Holyrood is helpful to present Christ to people who have yet to learn the faith. Margaret would make sure that people were properly converted. Also, she would correct what each church was teaching in error."

John asked, "So some churches have error? How?"

Edgar replied, "It's the way life is, John. You see, the more people there are, the more ideas that exist. Trying to get everyone to learn enough so that they worship and practice the faith correctly, and in the same way, is a difficult problem. Margaret tried very hard to encourage true worship. She had such a large effect on people wherever she traveled."

Martha said, "I know that many still speak very kindly about her."

Trip to Loch Ness

Edgar continued speaking. "There were a few times when I was able to travel with the king and queen, and there was one particular trip that I remember several things about. I shall tell you of when we went to the north in Scotland. One town there was so far north that the people felt scarcely part of Scotland, but when Malcolm talked with them and Margaret served Communion to them, the effect was to bring everyone together."

John asked, "Margaret was able to serve Communion?"

Edgar said, "Margaret was more priest than any priest I have ever known. She was amazing. She presented the Holyrood to the people and taught about the Savior's death and resurrection. When she was there, you didn't need a priest. Now this is why I remember this trip: there was a river that went through this town, and the river went to a long loch, this being the famous Loch Ness. And, yes, the people in the town insisted that there was a monster alive in the loch, or at least there was a story of a monster. So after our group had completed our meeting in the town, we determined to travel the trail beside the loch to see for ourselves. We had ridden our horses alongside the loch for a short time when our guide from the town pointed out toward the water and said, 'There is the evidence of the monster.' I looked and could see nothing. The guide exclaimed that I should look at the disturbance on top of the water. When I looked again, I could see that it appeared as if something had been swimming under the surface of the water, leaving a straight trail on the water's surface. As we rode our horses farther along the side of the loch, I noticed some more occasions when these curious, straight waves appeared, but we could see nothing causing them."

Edith, showing some excitement, approached Edgar to ask her question: "So, was there a monster?"

Edgar smiled weakly. "No, there is no monster. It was just the wind playing a trick on the water. So I told our guide that the wind was causing those lines on the water and that I had seen enough. We rode further until we reached a place to camp. The wind increased, the waves increased on the loch, and, of course, the trails vanished because of the waves. Our guide from the town explained that even if there were no monster in the loch, it still was useful to tell small children that a monster could come up out of the loch and snatch them away if they misbehaved." That started everyone laughing except for Edith. Edgar continued. "Even you children are old enough to know when someone is pulling the wool over your eyes. So if you want to tell your little ones that, you can create a monster in every loch, every pond, and every river in Scotland if it will help keep your little ones from misbehaving. But I did allow the guide this much: that while I have, on a few occasions, been able to see the wind play tricks on the surface of several lakes in Scotland, on Loch Ness this wind effect was rather easy to spot. In fact, it is almost common if the winds are right."

Edith, near tears, said, "Mother would tell me that there was a monster that would come out of the pond if I didn't fall asleep." The others suppressed laughter. Edgar sighed.

Martha said, "It is just for fun, Edith. We will tell your mother why you were upset when she comes."

Constance's Entrance

The door opened by the fireplace. William and Agnes appeared carrying a chair. The elderly Constance, wrapped in a blanket, was seated in the chair. Agnes said, "Edgar, here we have her."

Edgar had a concerned look on his face. "Constance, my good lady, let me look at you. Are you ailing?"

Constance was only able to talk quite slowly. "So good that you are here, Edgar. I was so anxious to see you again. I was so tempted to have stayed in bed. But you brought the Holyrood, so I said to myself, *It's all right; I will let them carry me.*"

William pointed to the case containing the Holyrood. "Here, Mother."

Constance turned. When she saw the cross-shaped case, she smiled. "There it is! Can you bring it to me?" William picked the cross out of the case and then placed it in Constance's hands once she slipped her hands outside the blanket. Constance was as delighted as someone who is ill could be. "This is wonderful!"

Edgar said, "I'm so cheered that we were able to bring this for you. But let me understand something: you were willing to come to church to see the Holyrood, but for me you would have stayed in bed?"

Constance waved her hand and replied, "Oh, Edgar, of course I want to see you. You always have to tease me. I see that you are alive and well."

Edgar said, "For a man past seventy years old, I am still fortunate to be alive."

Constance replied, "I'm older than you, and I think that I will be crossing the river to the other side soon." With a sigh, she continued, "You only live until you die, you were born to die."

William said, "Mother, please don't say such a thing."

Martha added, "Actually, Edgar, after we get her out of bed and give her some food and something to drink, she isn't as bad as she pretends."

Constance gazed longingly at the cross in her hands. "So beautiful to see again. And it's here at our new church. All right, I will say this, for all your sakes: this is helping me feel better."

John tried to offer encouragement. "You look better, Grandmother."

Constance nodded. "Yes, for now." She then turned to Edgar and asked, "What have you been working on, Edgar?"

Edgar replied, "I have been trying to help begin several churches, just as I have helped this church right here. Roadie—this is my driver, Roadie—will be taking me to another church after our lunch here. It will be a long Christmas Day for us."

Constance looked again at the Holyrood and said, "This reminds me of your family, Edgar."

Edgar decided to return to the previous topic of conversation. "Actually, I was telling everyone about Margaret and Malcolm just before you came in the door, Constance. Let me finish the story about Loch Ness." Once he had everyone's attention, he said, "That evening, we were camped by the loch. Margaret led our group in prayer. She prayed in the Spirit, so when she began to pray deeply, her words became indistinguishable. Now I can't even tell you what she said. I can only say that some of the things she spoke were only sounds."

Constance interrupted. "Margaret was my precious friend. I remember that she did that. It was amazing."

Edgar continued. "Then after speaking out loud what might be several sentences, she announced the interpretation of what she had said! I was silent, but I also was astonished. Others prayed aloud; some remained silent. Then, after the group were separating to sleep for the night, Margaret approached me directly. She said, 'Edgar, my brother, I have prayed for you so many times. Let me hold your hands.' So she took my hands and held them, and she talked to me for what seemed all night long. She asked me if I was remaining faithful. I, being much more concerned with the affairs of the kingdom and our conflicts, admitted that I really wasn't being very faithful. Finally, she said, 'Let me see if I can receive a word of prophecy for you.' She closed her eyes and prayed in the tongues of the Spirit. and then she stopped. Then she gave an interpretation. The best I can remember about it goes like this: 'Edgar, my son, I have loved you and I am holding you in my hands.' Again, I felt that this was amazing."

Constance spoke again. "I recall similar things about Margaret. She would pray with me too. Edgar, that is the way she was—and you couldn't stop her."

Edgar said, "Then Margaret challenged me to speak in tongues and pray in the Spirit. She said, 'Edgar, my brother, open your mouth and let the words out.' I felt nothing and remained silent. She placed her hands on top of my head. After a short while, I felt uncomfortable. I told her to stop and leave me alone. I am a man of strength, not weakness."

John exclaimed, "I have not heard of anything like this."

Edgar replied, "I have to say that it must be possible for a few people to pray in the Spirit. But time passed before I could determine that there was nothing wrong with me." Edgar paused. "Surely it is a mistake of nature when a man must have an older sister. And I had two older sisters. But Margaret could become so powerful in word." Edgar shook his head.

Constance asked, "Edgar, how long has been since Margaret has passed?"

Edgar replied, "It was, uh, about 1093, so she has been gone thirty, thirty-one years now."

Constance said, "Thirty-one years? Oh, you don't mean it? How the years have gone! We were together all the way back to Hungary. And I am even a year older than she."

John said to Edgar, "Sir, what you have said about this speaking in tongues is very amazing to me and the children. One of the children thought that the way you sound when you talk is speaking in tongues, but I told her no. Rather, that is just the accent you have when you speak."

This brought a bright smile to Edgar's face. "Accent? Why, I certainly have no accent." Pointing back toward the group of children, he added, "It is you who have an accent." This caused everyone to chuckle. "Now, I speak English perfectly. I speak English the way it is supposed to be spoken. And if you wanted me to speak French, I would speak French perfectly. If you asked me to speak Latin, I would speak Latin perfectly. I also grew up in Hungary, so if you asked me to speak the language of Hungary, I would speak that language perfectly. It is Italian that I stumble with a bit. Someone who is Italian would say that I have an accent. But everyone learns to speak a bit differently."

Andrus said to the children, "So do you now see why we can hold such respect for Edgar? He knows very many things."

barbara reed

Wade, Suzanne
& family -

Surprised to hear you
are moving!
The Web Site contains my
article on the Shroud of Turin
and some history of Barb's
family. Would like to

Know what you would think of the book as home school material. I still have some to give away.

I will miss seeing you guys a lot!

Al Reed

Edgar responded, "Oh, the world is so big that every time I see more of it, the more I realize that I really don't know that much. Even in English, all you have to do is travel a ways and soon you find that people speak English differently." It was a light utterance that caused everyone to chuckle.

The Shroud

John said to Edgar, "Sir, I have another question. My father says that in the Holy Land there is supposed to be a cloth that shows the very likeness of Christ. He also says that you have seen this artifact. Is this true?"

Edgar replied, "Oh, that is correct, and the cloth is miraculous! I have seen it, and it is unforgettable. The cloth is called a burial shroud, as it was wrapped around the body of Christ when the Savior was placed in the tomb. Then, when the resurrection occurred, the image of Christ was formed upon the cloth. The means by which the placement of this image was completed are completely miraculous. No one who has viewed the cloth can even imagine any natural means that would have caused this image to be created."

John asked, "Does the face of the Savior appear?"

Edgar answered, "Yes, the face is seen, but it is not like what we see when you and I look at each other's faces. There is almost no color on the shroud. And there is more. When you look very closely at the cloth, it is still possible to see items used in the crucifixion."

John asked, "How is that possible?"

Edgar replied, "The belief at the time was that items that had blood on them were to be placed with the dead. So the items used in the crucifixion were wrapped with Christ's body in the cloth. Then the resurrection placed the images of the items on the cloth."

John asked, "What items?"

Edgar answered, "The image that was the clearest was that of a sponge mounted on a stick. In the gospel, it is recorded that Jesus, while on the cross, said He was thirsty. So some Roman centurions put wine vinegar on a sponge that was attached to a stick and held the sponge up to Jesus' mouth so He could drink from it. You recall that part of the crucifixion story, correct? So, you see, the sponge and stick were required to be laid on the cloth, and the image of those two objects together now appears on the cloth. It was difficult to see many of the items on the shroud. A priest had to show me the cords the Romans used to scourge Jesus; the tip of the spear that was used to pierce His side; and an object by His head that was like the crown of thorns. Some flowers and plants can be seen. The wounds that Christ suffered are also seen. The wounds are marked by the blood that the Savior bled. The one that is most clearly seen is the spear wound on His side. But someone will show you everything on the cloth when you get there."

John asked, "I am in doubt. How can there be no color on the cloth? What do the items look like?"

"No, there is very little color. It is not like a painting. The items are like lines that appear on the cloth in much the same color as Christ," Edgar replied.

Andrus said to Edgar, "I wish that I had seen this cloth. Where is it now?"

Edgar said, "Constantinople. You have to go to Constantinople in the Byzantine Empire. The emperor himself will greet you and show the cloth when there is a group of people present."

William said, "The emperor himself? The emperor will greet you, Edgar, but not us fighting men. I did not get to see it."

Andrus said, "William, we did not try to see it. When we started back from the Holy Land after the Crusade, we sailed to Greece, then we traveled through Europe."

Edgar said, "That is where you missed it. Constantinople is on the overland route back from the Holy Land."

Andrus said, "We heard about this burial cloth, but then we did not believe that it would be shown to us."

Edgar replied, "If the emperor is not there, a priest will show the cloth. It will be shown to any group of knights and believers who desire to see it. Now listen to this: I have recently heard that a new fighting force of knights is being assembled on the continent and in the Holy Land. These men will be called the Knights Templar, and they will defend the Holy Land and provide protection for anyone who desires to make the pilgrimage. I believe that this will be important for the defense of the Holy Land and to preserving our victory. As I understand it, even you will be able to travel to the Holy Land and return."

William asked, "So I could return to the Holy Land and not have to be in an army myself?"

Edgar replied, "That is right. The whole family should be able to go."

Martha asked, "So could I go as well?"

Edgar answered, "Why, I believe, yes! Women and children can go as well!"

The children were excited. Edward volunteered, "I want to go!"

Andrus and William were much more subdued. Andrus said, "You people don't realize how far a trip it is to the Holy Land. Yes, it is a long trip! And where will there be food and shelter for this trip?"

Edgar said, "The food and shelter will be given by the Knights Templar as you journey. This will be part of the price that you pay for the trip."

Andrus said, "Ah, there's a cost for the trip. We will have to pay, William."

William shook his head. "No. I'm never going to see enough money in my whole life to be able to afford a trip like that!"

Edgar replied, "There certainly will be a cost, but let us try to find out what the trip actually will cost. Certainly it would be a helpful trip for John, as it would help him with his studies."

William was still frowning. "If we owned all the gold in the whole castle in Edinburgh, it still would not be enough for us to make this trip."

Edgar said, "You are teasing, of course. Again, let us find what the cost will be. It will depend on how you will travel."

Andrus said, "That is a fair question. Will we sail all the way there, or will we travel through the continent?"

William said, "It may be possible to sail there. That is what we did to get to the Crusade. But our boats were only good for firewood by the time we got there. It took us all winter long to make the trip. Our ship reached Antioch, not Jerusalem. And then how would we get to Constantinople?"

Edgar said, "You can sail to Constantinople. So I would say that it will be possible to sail there and see the shroud."

Andrus asked, "It's possible to sail to Constantinople? Then why didn't we sail there from the Holy Land?"

Edgar responded, "Constantinople is not in the best direction to sail from the Holy Land. That is why you sailed to Greece."

William and Andrus were both shaking their heads now. The rest of the group also showed evidence of confusion. Andrus offered, "It sure would be nice if anyone in the world could make some sort of a map."

Edgar said, "So you would like a map? John, do have a pen and something that I can mark upon?"

John got up and said, "I've got a pen and an extra sheet of paper near my Bible, so let me see if I can get them for you."

At this point, Constance spoke up, asking, "Edgar, do you remember that your father, Edward; your mother, Agatha; and several other people in Hungary went to Constantinople and saw the shroud?"

Edgar replied, "Now I remember that my mother did tell me about that a few times."

Constance said, "I recall that now. They did this before you were born. Now, Hungary is not that far from Constantinople. I believe that they took a boat down the Danube river."

Edgar said, "The Danube is a very big river. Going down the Danube is very good, but coming back up the river is quite a bit more difficult."

Edward asked, "If we traveled to Hungary, then could we get to the Holy Land?"

Andrus chuckled. "Do you realize how far it is from Scotland to Hungary? I don't even know where Hungary is. I just know it's a long way."

Edward asked Edgar, "Sir, can you tell us how far it is to the Holy Land?"

Edgar replied, "Young man, if I can write on something, I'll draw you a map."

John said, "A map is something that I would like to see. I can give you this pen, but I could only find a small paper. And why don't you show us, uh, on this table." John gave Edgar a pen and then set a table made of a very light-colored wood on top of a larger table. Edgar stood up, took the pen from John, and held part of the table steady. He made sure that everyone in the room could see the table.

Edgar said, "Good idea John. I think this will work Now let me show you how the land and sea can be seen." Edgar began sketching on the table and began to describe what he was sketching as people watched him. "Scotland is up in this corner, and the Holy Land is in the farthest corner. England is attached to Scotland." Edgar marked Scotland as *Sc,* England as *Eg.* and the Holy Land as *Holy.* "Jerusalem is in the Holy Land." Edgar drew each of these places as squares and then made a dot to mark Jerusalem, which he labeled with *Jer.* "France is larger than England, and Scotland and is shaped on several sides. Spain is below France." Edgar drew France so that it looked like a house. He then marked it as *Fr.* He drew Spain as a big square and marked it with *Sp.* Showing some frustration, Edgar then enlarged the areas of France and Spain. "I think these countries should be bigger. Now, Germany is next to France," he said, drawing a large oval marked *Ger.* "Hungary is past Germany," he said as he drew another large oval, this one marked *H.* "Italy is like this into the Mediterranean Sea." He drew a rectangle into the sea and marked it *It.* "Greece is about here, and there are many islands by Greece." As he said this, he drew a square and marked it *Gr.* He then drew another square to the right of Greece. "This is the center of the Byzantine Empire, and this is Constantinople." He indicated Constantinople with a *C* on the top left corner of this square. Looking back at his map, Edgar was again frustrated. "This isn't quite right because there is more land between Hungary and Constantinople. Now, you can sail to Constantinople because the Black Sea and the Mediterranean Sea are connected there." He drew a half oval for the Black Sea and marked it as *Sea.*

Brigette asked, "Does the Danube go close to Constantinople?"

Edgar replied, "The Danube ends in the Black Sea. It is still distant from Constantinople, but it is a good way to get to Constantinople. The river is about here." Edgar drew a line from Hungary to the Black Sea, marking the line as *DR.* Then he added several wavy lines to indicate all the seas.

Constance was the first to speak. "I remember the Danube from living in Hungary. It was so beautiful. I don't know about your map, but I love how this brings back so many memories of being a child in Hungary."

Andrew asked, "Sir, can you tell me how far it is to the Holy Land?"

Edgar took the smaller table and placed it on the floor in front of the children, who all eagerly gazed at it. He said, "I don't know how to describe how far it is to the Holy Land, but I do know that it's a long way. Maybe when we get to heaven, God will show us all the lands and seas."

Constance said, "We came all the way from Hungary to England and then Scotland with Margaret and Edgar and all their family. The Aethelings and the people we traveled with were the finest people ever put together. Edgar's father was such a wonderful man. Oh, how I wish that Edgar had been able to stay as king of England! Everything would have been so much better!"

Edgar sat down in his chair. "The kingdom was lost because of Harold and William the Conqueror. There is nothing we can do about it now."

Good Kings, Bad Kings

John spoke to Edgar. "Sir, we certainly have a good king now with David. I have met him several times. He has provided authority for us to build our church, as well as for others to build their own churches. And I understand that David is your nephew."

Edgar replied, "He is my nephew. David is an outstanding young man. He listens to what I tell him."

Andrus said, "David certainly cares about the churches. He was here, oh, about twenty days ago, I think. I believe he will be good for Scotland just the way Alexander and Edgar were before him."

Andrus's statement confused the children. Margie spoke out, saying, "Sir, I don't understand. Were you the king Edgar?"

Edgar smiled. "No, I wasn't that king Edgar. That was my nephew. He was named after me. But that Edgar, my nephew, died quite a few years ago. Then you had my nephew Alexander as king. You all remember him. He passed earlier this year, so now David. following after him, is king. And I sure hope David lives for a while. He is the last nephew I have left."

Margie was still confused. She asked, "Where did Edgar and Alexander and David come from?"

Edgar answered, "You remember that Malcolm and Margaret were the king and queen? We were talking about them a little while ago. Well, Margaret was my sister, and that is how I am related to all of them, Edgar, Alexander, and David. Malcolm and Margaret had eight children, and now only David is left. All of them have been very good for Scotland."

Andrus interrupted, saying, "They were all good except for that Edmund. He is the one who got mixed up with that Donald Bane."

The children were still confused. Andrew was the first to ask a question. "Did Edgar, your nephew, follow Malcolm? Who were the others?"

Edgar replied, "It would be a quite a long story to tell if I told you all about the whole family."

Constance said, "I remember that well, now that you mention Malcolm. Margaret died just a few days after Malcolm did, and their oldest son was killed down south somewhere while fighting the English. It caused the country to fall into confusion. Their second son was Edmund. He was supposed to be the king, but then that Irishman, Donald Ban or Bane, I don't know which, got together with Edmund and they tried to run the country together. Edmund was a fine young man, but Bane ruined him."

Andrus said, "This is when William and I joined Edgar's knights. We wanted to get rid of that Bane."

Constance said, "That lump of dirt, Bane, was trying to persuade the country to go back to the Gaelic language. Margaret had brought English to Scotland, and now this Bane was trying to go back to the old language. You can't go backwards. You can't have an Irishman running Scotland."

Andrus smiled. "So, you see, that is when Edgar, the former king of England, helped Edgar, the son of Malcolm and Margaret, become king of Scotland."

Everyone chuckled at this except for William, who was more grim. "Some of our knights really beat up on Bane. I started to feel sorry for him because he was old. But at the end, he deserved what he got."

Andrew was curious. "What happened to him?"

William replied, "He was beaten bad, and then they poked his eyes out." The women and children all winced.

Andrew asked, "What happened to him then?"

William answered, "Some people took him to their home to care for him, but he died a couple years later."

Edgar said, "In Donald Ban's, or Donald Bane's, honor, we have created two new expressions. These will be new words. The first expression is for Ban. Listen to this. A *ban* is when you don't want somebody or something. The other expression is just like it. A *bane* is someone you don't want because they are like a knife in your backside." Everyone chuckled at this.

Andrew still wanted to sort this out. He said, "So Edgar and Alexander were good kings. And David is now a good king. But before that, we had Donald, and he was bad. And Edmund was king with Donald?"

Andrus answered, "That's right. Edmund tried to rule with Bane, but we didn't like it. Now they are both gone."

Andrew asked, "Did Edmund get killed?"

Andrus replied, "No, he wasn't killed. He just died. We weren't mad at Edmund. It was Bane who was ruining him."

Andrew asked, "Then before Donald and Edmund we had who?"

Constance spoke next. "Malcolm was king, but I have to tell you, Queen Margaret was the one running the country. Malcolm just liked his drink. He would go off to England to fight and try to capture slaves. Margaret was the one getting things done. She could make Malcolm agree with her about anything except attacking England. She told him not to go attack England, but Malcolm went to fight England anyway—and that was the end of him. That's how he caused his own undoing."

Andrew asked, "So Malcolm and Margaret together were good?"

Edgar replied, "Yes, absolutely. They were a good king and queen."

Andrew asked, "Who were all their family?"

Edgar answered, "Well, let me see. Edward was the first, and he was killed with Malcolm. Edmund was second. Then there was Aethelred. But there was something about him. Aethelred was never going to amount to anything. Then Edgar, Alexander, and David. Those are the men. Then there were the girls, Edith and Mary. Edith married King Henry of England. But they are both gone now too."

Constance nearly cried. "O Lord, I can't imagine that they are all gone save for David and you. Oh my God."

John asked, "Is Henry still king of England?" Edgar nodded his head yes. "Is he a good king?"

Edgar reflected. "Well, yes, if you believe that your king should be an adulterer," he said.

Constance retorted, "Henry is an adulterer? He was such a nice little boy when I knew him. How can you say that he is an adulterer?"

Edgar replied, "It's very easy to say that he is an adulterer because everyone around him knows it is true. He has children by other women. And this happened even when Edith was still alive." Constance shook her head in disbelief.

John asked, "So, otherwise, is Henry a good king?"

Edgar replied, "I don't think Scotland has anything to be concerned about. Henry is too concerned with his own pleasure. He continues to levy heavy taxes upon the people."

Andrus asked, "So, Edgar, what makes a king good?"

Edgar paused. After a few moments, he said, "A good king keeps his nation at peace and wins the wars that he has to win. Any king that can manage even that is going to be a good and lucky king. And a king that loses a war could still be a good king, but one that just happens to lose, which means that he may not be king anymore. A bad king will exhaust his people by starting wars and heavily taxing his subjects."

When Edgar Was King

John, making an effort to help Edgar engage the children, asked, "Sir, can you explain to us how long ago you were the king of England?"

Edgar said, "How long ago? Ah, here is a chance for you young ones to practice your education. Do you young ones know how I keep that date? What is today? Today is Christmas. On Christmas Day in 1066, I had to watch William take the crown that I should have possessed. So from 1124 to 1066 is how many years? Can you answer that?"

Andrew and Edward looked at each other and began counting. Edward finally answered, "Fifty-eight years." Most of the people marveled at Edward's answer.

Edgar replied, "You are correct! It was fifty-eight years ago today that I had to watch the William the Conqueror take my place, my rightful place, as king of England. A way to get the number is by doing this: 1124 to 1100 equals twenty-four years, and 1066 to 1100 equals thirty-four years, so if you add twenty-four and thirty-four, then your sum is fifty-eight years. Do you kids follow that? If you are learning how many eggs make six, you should know that. You had better."

Andrew thought for a moment and said, "I will write that down, sir."

John asked Edgar, "Sir, could you explain what happened when you were king? The children and I don't understand the history."

Andrus added, "This is something I don't understand either, as this happened long before our memory."

Edgar responded, "It is a really a long story, but here are the facts that can be remembered. The king of England Edward the Confessor died. They called him 'the Confessor' because he was believed to be very faithful. I was next to become king because I was in the family line, but instead of choosing me, the English nobles named Harold king."

Andrew said, "Sir, that was bad to name another man king."

Edgar responded quickly, "No, it was good that I did not become king then. Harold was experienced in the leadership of the army."

Andrew asked, "So when did you become king?"

Edgar answered, "This is when William the Conqueror from Normandy invaded. In the battle, Harold was killed. After that happened, I was named king."

Andrew asked, "What was it like to be king? Did you get to wear a big crown on your head?"

Edgar replied, "Ah, young children, no, I did not. Every day I continued to ask the men around me when could I have my coronation ceremony. The coronation is when the crown is placed on the king's head. And every time I asked, they would always put me off. They would say, 'No, we can't do that, because it would make William angry.' I would say, 'It does not matter what William thinks. I should be the king.' They would say, 'If we gave you the crown, then your life would be in danger.' I would say that they would protect me. But they would say that they could not protect me. And then they would tell me that if I were crowned, then William would likely have me killed if he were able to catch me. If I remained uncrowned, they said, then William would allow me to live."

Andrew asked, "What did you do when you were king?"

Edgar thought for a moment. "Young man, I am at a loss to tell you anything, because I really did nothing. Every day I met with the landowners and the leaders of the cities and towns. And the army leaders. Every day I would listen to them say that the Norman army was advancing toward London. Someone would say that the Normans had entered a town and that they had killed some men. Someone would report that in another place they looted goods and stole food. Then another would report that they had entered his land and taken his horses and butchered some of his sheep and chickens. Another would say that he had heard of where the Normans had entered a store and taken money. And then I would ask these people what they were doing to stop the Normans. They would continue to insist that our army was no longer together after the Battle at Hastings. The army didn't have enough men left to stop the Normans."

Constance added, "So, you see, after a short time Edgar had to give up being king because of William. That William the Conqueror was not a great man. He had men killed because he was a thief."

William the Conqueror's Relics

Edgar began to mock William the Conqueror. He said, "William the Conqueror. Here is what that snake would say." With an attempt at a French accent, Edgar started speaking slowly. "The Norman and the Englishman will work together, side by side." He shook his head before starting again. "Edgar, you and I will lead hand in hand to bring justice to England and Scotland." Edgar winced.

Constance responded, "That's right. He lied. He was as cunning as the Devil himself."

Resuming speaking in his normal voice, Edgar asserted, "Power and money was all he ever cared about. He was a filthy scoundrel. He didn't care who he trampled or how many men he had to crush. It's good that we are in a church, as it prompts us to restrain our words. Here is something that I think you have never heard about. William wanted me to swear my allegiance to him. I saw no choice but to promise that I would be loyal to him. Then he brought out a certain box. I had already heard about the box, and I told him so. I then told him that I was not going to swear an oath over his dirty box of relics. When he realized that I already knew about his box and that it would accomplish nothing more with me, he opened the box and let me see me his collection of relics."

Andrew spoke up and asked, "Sir, what are relics?"

Edgar replied, "You have not heard of relics? Relics are human bones. William had quite a collection in this box."

Andrew asked, "Human bones? From people that are dead?"

Edgar nodded. "Yes. A number of dead people."

Margie asked, "Were there any skulls?"

Edgar nodded again. "Yes. Several skulls."

The children were astonished. Edward asked, "Who were the people?"

Edgar replied, "The bones were from his ancestors and from saints. Well, he said they were from saints, but I don't believe that any one of his ancestors is going to be a saint. His relatives were all a bunch of thieves."

Edith paced nervously. Edward asked, "So were the skulls from people that he knew?"

Edgar replied, "That is something that I don't know, who were the people in his box. If he knew who they were, which skulls and which bones of his belonged to which one of each of his ancestors, I did not know. He might have had them marked."

Andrus asked, "How did you know that there were relics in the box?"

Edgar replied, "I knew because I had heard the story of his relics. I knew this because I had heard of something that had happened. Let me tell you this story. Harold was a man who had become friends with the king Edward the Confessor. Because of this, Harold was the next in line to be king of England, even ahead of me. That is why Harold was named king after Edward died. Well, listen to this: One day, Harold and a companion of his went out on a boat to fish in the North Sea. A wind blew up and they could not steer the boat. Their boat blew all the way to the beach in Normandy. Some people in Normandy found them and took them to William. So there they were, Harold, the Englishman who wanted to be the king of England, and William, the Norman who wanted to be the king of England. They both knew each other and knew that they were rivals. And William had Harold at his mercy." Edgar held his hands to indicate strangling. "William had an idea. William made this promise to Harold, that he would help get him and his boat back to England, but first Harold had to give his oath to William, swearing that when King Edward was out of the way, Harold would help him, William, become king of England. Well, Harold was stunned, of course. However, William assured Harold that there was no way out otherwise. So Harold gave his oath to William. But this didn't conclude the matter for William. He decided that Harold should get down on his knees and give his oath. Harold was once again stunned. Still seeing no other way, Harold knelt down and repeated his oath. But William wasn't done yet. He brought out his box of relics and placed it in front of Harold. He told Harold to repeat his oath while kneeling and placing his hands on the box, as this would help William become king of England. Harold probably thought that the box was an altar, so he, again reluctantly, repeated the oath. After this, William opened the box and showed the relics to Harold.

"When William told me this story, he and his sons began to laugh and laugh. He said that when Harold saw the relics and skulls inside the box, William's sons could not tell which was more white: the bones or Harold's face!" Edgar and the adults laughed. Edith paced nervously.

Edward asked, "What happened then?"

Edgar replied, "William helped Harold get back to England. But it would be just a year later when the two would meet again. Well, maybe they didn't meet, but they did stand across from each other at the Hastings battlefield. At the battle, William was victorious. Harold was killed."

Edward asked, "So did the relics work?"

Edgar replied, "No, the relics were meaningless. What worked for William was the Norman army fighting harder and better than the English army."

Andrew asked, "Why didn't William kill Harold when he had a chance?"

Edgar answered, "You cannot kill an enemy in a time of peace. If William had killed Harold, then the people of England would have been so angry that they would have gone to war. It would have been a senseless killing. There would have been so much resentment and anger toward William that he would not have had a chance to become king."

Constance said, "I remember that story, Edgar. That William the Conqueror was nothing but a dirty dog. Children, this was the time when Edgar was the king of England, after Harold and the English army were lost at this battle. Edgar was king, so respect him and listen to what he says."

Would You Be A King?

Andrew said to Edgar, "Sir, it's too bad that you did not get to stay being king."

Edgar thought for a moment and then replied, "No, it is a good turn that I did not stay king. Do you know what would have happened to me if I tried to stay king?" Edgar's eyes widened. He looked at Andrew. "Young man, should you like to be king?"

Andrew thought for a few seconds and then replied, "Well, it seems like everyone would like to be king."

Edgar asked him, "You would?" Then he looked to Edward and asked him the same question: "Would like to be king?"

Edward thought and then replied quietly, "I guess so."

Edgar looked at John. John volunteered by saying, "A king is rich, and everyone wants to be rich."

Edgar leaned back slightly, surveying all of the young people in the room. "And all of you would like to be king, I suppose?"

The room was silent. Now no one wanted to answer Edgar's question. They anticipated his next words. No one dared guess what Edgar would say to them next.

Edgar slowly stood up and finally spoke. "Young man, you should not wish to become a king. Do you realize what will happen when you are king?" Edgar let his words settle for a few seconds. "Young man, if you are king, everyone will try to *kill* you!"

Everyone was stunned and silenced by Edgar's stern pronouncement.

Edgar began again. "How many stories would you like to hear? Listen, listen to this experience. When I was in Italy and heard about the death of William the Conqueror, I returned to Normandy only to find that there was conflict even within William's family as to who would be king. Before he died, William left word that his second son, who was also named William, should be the king. I knew William's oldest son, Robert, very well, and Robert thought that he should be king. Robert asked for my help, and so I began to help him to try to overthrow his brother William. Can you picture that? One brother is king and the other wants to be king, so I am helping one brother try to overturn the other. Brother against brother! Do you see that? But see this: even I have had thoughts of murder. My rightful place on the English throne could only be reclaimed if we English could rid ourselves of William. After that, I could deal with Robert. My friend Robert. But I would never get that far.

"One night, Robert began to tell me about the way he had been passed over by William to succeed his father to the throne. Of course, he was very bitter about this. As Robert was William's oldest son, he felt entitled to the throne. But then he pointed at me and said, 'Edgar, do not get any ideas that you will ever be king again, for my brother William and I will not destroy each other as your family have done to each other.' I asked what he meant by that. He replied, 'Edgar, don't you realize that it was your great-uncle Edmund who had your father murdered?'"

Constance now summoned as much energy as she could. She protested, "Edgar, I have never heard you blame your father's death on Edward the Confessor."

Edgar retorted quickly, "This is just what Robert was telling me. I don't know what exactly happened to my father."

Constance replied with, "Your father was a great man. He should have been king. We would have been so much better off. And Edward was a very fine man."

Edgar said, "Let me return to the story. I told Robert that I had always been suspicious of what had happened. Robert persisted, saying, 'When your father arrived in England, Edward was, of course, interested to see what kind of a man he was exactly. And he was embarrassed, for your father had a strange accent and could scarcely speak the English language. So your father had to go. How could a man who could scarcely speak the English language be king of England? And Edmund was always pleased to eliminate any potential competition for his throne. Let me tell you something else: it was your uncle who had those three Vikings murdered before he became king. There was no way he was going to be king unless he got rid of them, those three, Cnut the Viking and his two sons. He got them all in the 1040s. And he got them one right after another until he was king.'

"I asked Robert, 'How do you know this?' He replied, 'Edward told my father all about his exploits. He boasted about all of these killings. And my father passed this along to us—when you had gone away somewhere else, of course.'

"I said, 'Edmund was known as the Confessor, as an extremely religious man.' Robert laughed. He then said, 'Edgar, he had to be the Confessor because he was always confessing to all the murders he had committed! His religion was only for show, to impress others. He has been gone for twenty years now, but I'll bet he is not in heaven yet. He is in purgatory now, still trying to get forgiven!'

"I said that I knew Edmund was not present when my father died. Robert replied, 'He didn't have to be there, as he had other people do his deeds for him. It was easy to do, seeing as there were other men who wanted to be king. One of the men who helped do in your father was William St. Clair.' I immediately protested. 'William St. Clair? The Seemly One?' I asked. 'He was the man who came to Hungary and brought us to England. He would have been in my father's court. He came to Scotland and remained a friend of my family. He would not have turned on us.'"

Constance jumped on this. "William St. Clair was a wonderful man and our friend."

Edgar glanced toward Constance to respond. "But this is just Robert's story. Robert claimed, 'All St. Clair knew about it was just getting your father to England. He was our relative, you know, and he was going to gain when my father became king. Of course he may have had gain even if your father had become king, but this was an extra chance for him. But your father was an outsider; he really didn't have a chance. And the Confessor, besides being a murderer, was a liar. He enjoyed making promises to different men, even saying that they could follow him to the throne. That is why he was popular, because he gave so many promises that sounded good. But then, of course, he couldn't keep them all.' After I heard that, I just sat still. Was Robert being truthful? Or was he a braggart who was boasting, his tongue unloosed by the ale we had been drinking? I think it was the drinking that made him senseless. I am left with suspicions that I cannot resolve. But I have put all this out of my mind and left it behind me."

William had stirred when he heard the word *ale.* Now he stood from his chair. "When you said *ale,* that reminded me of something I've got to get for you, Edgar."

Agnes was resistant to William. "Oh, William, please don't bring that stew of yours here."

William retorted, "Edgar will enjoy this." He then turned and walked out of the door.

Constance again summoned her energy. "Again I will say that your father was a great man. All of us who came from Hungary loved him. And, children, Edgar was even younger than all of you when his father died."

Edgar slowly moved to another place in the room and began to speak again. "What happened years later? Someone murdered William, after which the throne of England was given to Henry, the next son of William the Conqueror. When this happened, Robert and I were in the Holy Land in the Crusade. Robert was passed over for the throne again, so when we returned from the Holy Land, what do you think happened? Robert and I were trying to overthrow Henry. Brother against brother again!" Edgar paused. "But back to you, young man! Now do you still want to be king? What do you have to say now?" Edgar drew his sword. "Do you know what they say in Germany? They have a word that sounds like this: *sska-put!* Do you know why they say 'sska-put'?" Edgar waved the sword in the air and then brought the blade of the sword up to the boy's neck. "The *sska* sound is for the sword slashing toward the neck. Then the *put* is the sound of the head hitting the floor." Edgar now showed an evil smile. "Sska-put! That's it, the end for you: sska-put!" This caused everyone to recoil.

Edgar continued. "So now, young man, do you think that you should try to kill your father, or your brother or a cousin or an uncle or a friend, to become a king?" Edgar allowed the sword to hang at his side. He looked up. "I used most of my life trying to take back my rightful place as king of England. And now do you realize what would have happened to me had I actually returned to the throne? Why, certainly I would have been sska-put—a long time ago!" Edgar brought the blade of the sword to his neck and looked directly at John. "Sska-put! Only now in my old age do I realize that had I been king, I would have been disposed of under a stone a long time ago." Edgar began to return his sword to its scabbard. "If you want to be a king that stays alive for long, you must have many friends and a large family who have your back and neck protected from the knife. And your cupbearer, the man who watches over your food and drink, must be absolutely trustworthy to keep your cup free from the poison that would take your breath away. I would not have been able to last long as king. So now, in my old age, I thank the Almighty daily for my life and His blessings. For the Lord has protected me and has allowed me to live this long life, and He has shown me what I now know. This is a great day for your church, which the almighty Lord has allowed me to live to see. It does not matter if you are a king or not a king. You are filling the Almighty's purpose for your life no matter what you are doing."

War and Emotions

Edgar put his sword all the way into his scabbard and slowly sat down. He began to speak again. "You young men will have enough trouble in this life. Soon you will be carrying a sword and a shield. Now you should pray that fortune will shine on you, that you may not have to go into battle. But you have a long time ahead of you. You all, I should fear, will be carrying a sword and a shield someday."

Edith began to cry. Agnes began to comfort her. "Come here, Edith. Why should you cry?"

Edith replied through her sobs, "Because Edward will have to go to war."

Agnes, still trying to comfort Edith, said, "Oh, he will not go to war. If we are faithful to pray, there will be no more wars."

William returned carrying a small bottle and three small cups on a tray. He said, "Now, Edgar, I've got something to share with you. You are going to like this." William set the cups on the table and began to pour liquid into the cups.

Edgar watched as William poured the first cup. He said, "The color looks very fine." William gave the cup to Edgar and went to pour the other two cups.

Edgar held the cup to his nose for a moment and then commented, "Ah, this is very promising." William had filled his own cup and had sat down next to Edgar. When Edgar held his cup out, the two men touched their cups together and then proceeded to drink. After finishing the drink, William simply set his cup down and smiled, but Edgar allowed his eyes to open very wide. He puckered his lips and made a smacking sound with his tongue. Finally, Edgar commented, "Woo-ee, William, you have fire in liquid here!"

William replied, "Isn't that something? And I made this!"

Edgar replied, "William, I think you have something here. You have made Scotland proud. Men will like to have their names on this drink."

William asked, "So who would like the third cup? Edgar, how about one more?"

Edgar replied, "No, William, this will make me a little crazy. When I get started, I can get into an argument. I remember my life and I become sad much more than glad."

William asked, "Andrus, how about this one?"

Andrus declined, saying, "No, thanks, William. We are going to eat soon."

William said, "Well, John isn't going to drink it."

Edgar then turned to Roadie. "Hey, Roadie. Take this." Edgar held the cup toward Roadie.

Roadie replied, "Oh, I'm not sure, sir."

William goaded the driver. "Come on, Roadie. It will put some hair on your chest and whiskers on your chin." This caused everyone to chuckle. Roadie took the cup from Edgar. He held it for a moment, then moved away from William toward the door.

Edgar asked William, "So how did you come up with this?"

William replied, "It is not hard to make. The real question is why I make this. The answer is because it helps me sleep."

Edgar evidenced surprise. "This drink helps you sleep?" In the background, Roadie took a sip of the drink. He reacted by putting his sleeve over his mouth and trying to spit out the liquid as quietly as he could. But Edgar noticed. "A great drink, right, Roadie?"

Roadie replied in a muted voice, "Delightful, sir." But Roadie had succeeded in not being noticed by anyone else.

William continued. "Edgar, I take about three or four of these every night before I go to bed."

Edgar was shocked. "You have three or four of these? I can see where that will knock you down."

William said, "When you talk about these kings being killed and the use of the sword, it brings back memories. When I go to bed at night, I have so many memories. I keep seeing the same things. Even Martha knows that I have memories that are troubling. Seeing what we saw in battle, the dead and the dying, is a frightful memory for me. That is why I take the drink."

Edgar nodded in agreement. "Sometimes the best thing is to talk it over. Get it out of yourself."

William said, "First, there is the tremendous excitement as the two forces meet, the noise of swords and spears clashing, the arrows whooshing all around, and all the men shouting, everyone trying to be louder than the other. Then men start falling all around. Some are bleeding, others are dying, and some lie dead right where they fell. But the worst is when it is all over. Then it is quiet and I walk around looking at those bodies. There is blood all over every man. I see the insides of men cut out of them. There are fingers, hands, arms, and even heads lying separated from the bodies. I remember their faces, some of the men who were my friends and who are now gone forever. And there is a dreadful smell with death. Oh my God. I sure hope war is over forever, but I'm afraid it will never go away." In the back of the church, Roadie cracked the door open just enough to toss the rest of his drink away and not be noticed by the adults. The children saw him do this and suppressed their smiles.

Edgar brought his hands together as if to pray. "I saw my first battle a long time ago. And many more since then."

William nodded in agreement. "Do you know what worked the best? I tell you it was the big spears. A man with an ax or a sword mostly just beats on the outside of his opponent. Arrows are hit-and-miss, mostly miss. But take one of those big spears and you can really run it through the man you're fighting against. Nothing better than being on a horse with a big spear. With the ax or sword, you are just trying to make a big hole in your opponent, but you're probably not getting through him. I say to take the spear and run him through. Best is to start at a point and push the hole in the man so it becomes bigger and bigger."

Agnes and Martha became progressively more impatient as William spoke. Finally, Agnes interrupted him. "Oh, you men, why do have to talk about this? This is awful!"

William answered, "But this has been our life."

Agnes continued her complaint: "We get fish and we cut their heads off and slice their guts. We get a deer or a lamb or a chicken and we kill them and then we butcher the meat. But we don't carry on talking about the insides and blood we have spilled."

William scarcely noticed Agnes' words. He said to Edgar, "Edgar, do you remember the battle cry of 'Make the streets of Jerusalem run red in blood'? I was one who tried to make that happen."

Agnes was emotionally spent. "Oh, you men!" she said before she buried her face in her hands for a moment.

The children were wide-eyed at this point. Martha was calm. She said, "I have heard you say these things before, so, children, don't be concerned. This will not happen again. We must have hope that one day soon, men will become civilized."

Edgar continued, saying, "William, you are quite correct about the damage weapons will do to a man." He pointed to his chest. "Better is the weapon that makes a small hole going in and a big hole coming out the other side than a weapon that makes a big hole on the front and only a small hole going through. You are quite right."

"Better is the weapon that makes a small hole going in and a big hole coming out the other side than a weapon that makes a big hole on the front and only a small hole going through." *Westbow Press Illustration*

Edgar paused very briefly before speaking again. "Every battle is different. And at the end of every battle, the dead lie on the ground, each body in its own position. The arms can be one way, the legs their own way, the head in its own way. Every body that is fallen looks different. And I'll tell you something else. When you look at the faces of the dead, you can tell who believed in Christ and who didn't believe. The unbelievers don't change a bit. They look just they did when they were alive. But when a Christian dies, his appearance changes. The passing of a Christian takes the soul of that person away—and you can tell the difference. My example of that was my sister Margaret, the queen, for her face became radiant when she passed into the next life. And I know more like this!"

Edgar's Dreams

William stated, "I even have dreams about battle, but I forget them right away. But they still trouble me. And you, Edgar, when we used to be at rest for the night, you would wake us up with your shaking and mumbling. It appeared as if you were fighting yourself as you slept."

Andrus smiled slightly. "We never wanted to sleep too close to you, Edgar, for we were afraid that you would grab a sword and swing it in the middle of the night."

Edgar replied, "But you are right. Do you know what I have dreams about? I have had dreams many nights that have wakened me in a sweat. Do you children entertain each other by telling one another about your dreams?"

The children glanced quickly at one another. Andrew answered, "Just a little."

Margie then volunteered her dream. "I have had a dream about my sheep. I love my sheep, but in my dream my favorite sheep named Beck ran and tried to bump me. Beck tried to run over me. I told Beck to stop. But Beck continued to try to bump me. Then I woke up and I was still saying 'Beck, stop it, stop it.' Then I knew that I just had a dream."

Edgar started again. "Young lady, you must have a rebellious sheep there. Probably he just wants you to pet him some more. But I remember having dreams that frightened even me. One dream that occurred to me over and over until it went away was this: I was with a group of soldiers. Riding horses, we were entering a forest of trees. But soon after we rode into the forest, the other soldiers began riding in different directions. Soon I was alone. I took out my sword. As I rode by trees, I would slash their bark where they stood until I had slashed several trees. I stopped at one tree and slashed it, but I could find no marks on it. I rode back to the other trees I had struck, but I could find no marks on any of them. I stopped my horse at one tree and struck it many times with my sword, but to no effect. Then I said to myself, 'Surely if I strike a limb, my sword will cut it.' So I struck at a limb that was over my head and growing straight out of the tree. I struck it many times, but the strikes had no effect. I said, 'Surely I can cut a small branch,' but again my sword could not cut even a small branch. Then I tried swinging wildly at the leaves of the tree, but the leaves just slid off my sword. Then I looked down to find that another horse was biting my horse and my armor!" This last utterance drew a stunned reaction from several of the family.

Edgar continued. "I suffered another dream that came from the time I was trapped in a shipwreck. I was in the ocean with high waves all around. A huge fish was coming toward me. I began to think, *Will I have to spend three days in the belly of this fish?* But then I saw that the fish had huge teeth. I would never get into the belly of the fish past those teeth! Then I thought, *Someone has already spent three days in the belly of a fish! I will not have to do that!* So I kicked my legs and arms, and soon I was in the air above the sea! The fish could jump out of the water but could not get me. I believe this dream has occurred to me because I survived the shipwreck." This caused a reaction of relief from everyone.

Constance sighed. "Thank God," she said.

Edgar said, "Do you believe that I am bringing some sort of shame on myself by telling you my dreams? No, I am not. I have endured far more shame than this. Let me teach you this: dreams are a way for your mind to release the great force of your thoughts. Even the Bible tells us about dreams and their interpretation. But do you know what? I have not had these dreams for a long time. I have felt peace for a good, long time now. Just like a river flows, the dreams have run their course. You see, William, it is better to talk about the things that you have seen that are troubling your mind. By telling us these things, you will find relief for your mind."

Constance added, "William, remember that time heals all things."

Edgar corrected her: "That is precious. Time can help you forget or forgive something. That may not heal you, may not restore what you were before, but you will become more peaceful as the memories fade. But always remember, it is God who is the healer. This is why the Bible says to offer confessions to one another. The confession as well as something as crazy as a dream is all part of the many ways God will help you feel better."

The Jews

Andrus stated, "Another memory that I have is about the Jews. Some of the other Crusaders were talking about killing Jews. I wondered what the sense of that would be."

Edgar replied, "I remember that very well. I went to the commander of those Crusaders and began to implore that man to put a stop to such inhumanity. This man proceeded to spit in my face!" Edgar paused. What he had said surprised everyone. "So I hit his face with my fist as hard as I could. We were separated by men standing next to us."

Andrus was most surprised by this. He said, "What happened? I did not hear that you were in such a fight."

Edgar replied, "Oh yes! I told him that our Crusade is for the Holy Land, not just to kill people. He shouted back to me that it is right for us to kill Jews, for they are the haters of Christ. I shouted back that it is not our judgment to make. I set about finding several of his men. Once I found them, I gave them orders not to kill the Jews or to take any life unless it was necessary in a battle. But some of the men argued with me, so it became necessary for me once again to raise my voice with them. I ordered them not to kill again unless in a battle."

William recalled, "There was so much hatred of Jews. I thought everyone was supposed to hate Jews."

Andrus, looking at Edgar, stated, "We did not kill any of them because of your orders."

Edgar replied, "That is good. Since that time, I have had many chances to think about that occasion. When that incident happened, I immediately recalled the words of William the Conqueror, who told me, 'You can't lead by lifting the heads off of everyone that you don't like.' I was surprised that the words of my enemy the Conqueror occurred to me at that very moment. And yet now I can fully understand what his point was, for he certainly had any number of chances to take the heads of many Englishmen, including me and my family, had he so determined. And why didn't William carry out such annihilation? Because William realized that further bloodshed would be the cause of further and deeper hatred. A leader must realize the consequences and the counteraction that people would take, or even be forced into, if conflict and killing were extended. It is a necessity to kill in battle, but it is much different to take a life without cause. This is as sure as the sixth commandment in the Bible, 'Do not kill.' So while I restrained our men not to kill Jews, I know that this happened elsewhere in the Crusade."

Andrew raised his arm. "Sir, who are the Jews?"

Edgar answered, "The Jews are people just as we are. The difference is that they have not believed in Christ."

Andrew asked, "So why don't they believe in Christ?"

Edgar replied, "That's a difficult question to answer. Jesus Christ came into the world as a Jew, and yet many Jews did not accept Him."

Edward asked, "Are there very many Jews?"

Edgar replied, "There are a large number of Jews."

Edward inquired, "Are there Jews in Scotland?"

Edgar answered, "I think there is small number here. There are more Jews in Europe and closer to the Holy Land."

John said, "I believe that Jews will say that Jesus did not follow their laws and traditions. But I cannot understand this hatred. Why would they be hated such that Crusaders would want to kill them?"

Edgar responded, "I don't understand this either, John. The Jews are despised even by the heathens who occupy the lands and countries that are in and around the Holy Land. The heathens regard the Jews as possessing homes, livestock, land, and money that the former think should belong to them. The Jews are pressed on all sides, but still they survive. So, what are we to think about the Jews? Are they still the chosen people of God? Can they still be chosen even after Jesus Christ, the Messiah, has come? The Scripture gives evidence that there will still be Jews who are alive and practicing their beliefs at the time when Christ returns. Surely the Almighty has a purpose for this, one that remains a mystery to us. At some future time, we can expect a great change in the beliefs of people throughout the world."

Lions

After a pause, Andrus asked, "Do you remember the nights in the Holy Land when we were wakened by the awful sound of the lions?"

Edgar replied, "Oh, of course, how could I or anyone who heard that roar forget the lions? We would be roused from our sleep by the most ungodly of noises. I suppose that it is like the sound of an earthquake. We thought at first that the lions were close by, but we could not see them. Then one day I saw a lion far away, and I saw it open its mouth wide and make this horrible roaring noise. I could not believe how far away it was—and still I heard it."

One of the children spoke up, asking, "What did the lion sound like?"

Edgar replied, "I can't repeat it—maybe something like, *Rrr*." The children tried to imitate the sound.

Andrus said, "I'm very glad that being wakened by lions only happened a few times. But then one morning after we had heard some roaring the night before, some people from a small town came and said"—Andrus tried to imitate the accent of people attempting to speak English—"Please come and kill the man-eating lion."

Andrew asked Edgar, "Sir, our father has told us this 'man-eating lion' story several times. Did you get to see that?"

Edgar replied, "I did hear about that, and I ordered our soldiers not to go lion hunting. I told them that it was too dangerous and that we should not waste our time and strength. Some archers in another group went out and were able to chase the lion away, but they gave up when they saw how fast the lion was able to get away. But I was able to see a lion very closely. It was in Constantinople, on my way back from the Holy Land. There was a small arena where the lion was held captive."

William sighed. "Oh, now we have to go to Constantinople to visit the lion?"

Andrus added, "Surely we traveled the wrong way back from the Holy Land." Andrus and William gave each other a wry smile. The children, however, seemed anxious to make the trip.

Edward said, "Let's go to the Holy Land!"

Edith said, "I want to see the lion."

Andrew asked, "But how could any animal be large enough to eat a man?"

Edgar stood up and used his hands to help create an image to accompany his description. "The lion is as long as this table—maybe even longer than this table—and its tail makes it even longer."

The children were amazed when Edgar described the size of the lion. Edward asked, "How can you catch an animal like that and keep it alive?"

Edgar answered, "I suppose that you could catch a lion while it is still small. That would be the easiest. It might be possible to trap a full-size lion, but that would be quite a struggle. But in Constantinople, the lion is kept in a stone enclosure surrounded with high walls. I watched as they fed the lion a large piece of meat. I could see that it had huge teeth—those two huge fangs that start from the top and front of its mouth. When I saw this beast up close, I was amazed at its size. It is plenty large enough to eat a man. Did you know that, way back in the early days of the Roman Empire, Christians were crucified and were actually fed to lions?"

Andrew asked, "People were fed to lions? How is that possible?"

Edgar responded, "You have not heard of the brutality of the Romans, but, of course, one has to study history to know about what happened. After the crucifixion of Christ, but before the time of the emperor Constantine, the Romans persecuted Christians. The Romans had large arenas where thousands of spectators could sit in seats above the floor. The spectators would be entertained by whatever was occurring on the floor. Say the Romans had captured some Christians in order to persecute them. What is supposed to have happened is that these people were brought out to the floor of the arena, at which time hungry lions would be released."

This brought a reaction from everyone in the family. Martha asked, "So these Romans actually watched the lions eat these good people?" Edgar nodded affirmatively. "And Christians were crucified as people watched?" Edgar nodded again.

William said, "I heard the lions while I was in the Holy Land, and that was enough."

Andrew said, "I can barely imagine that. It sounds terrible. It's good that I can scarcely imagine such a scene."

John asked Edgar, "Sir, have you learned much about Constantine? Knowing about him is part of my training to become a priest, but there is not much written about his life."

Edgar responded, "John, about all I know about Constantine is that he was the first Roman emperor who became a Christian. He ended the practices of crucifying people and of throwing people to lions. Because of Constantine, the church, and indeed all of civilization, changed greatly for the better."

Edith asked, "Are there lions in Scotland?"

Edgar barely cracked a smile. He said, "Oh, no. There are no lions here. If there were lions here, you would know it." Edgar looked to the floor and saw Tat the house cat tied to the table. He pointed to the cat and said, "The people in the Holy Land told us that the lion is the same kind of animal as that cat lying right there."

Edith spoke next. "Sir, this Tat, Tat the cat. He is very friendly."

Andrew chimed in. "Yes, very friendly, when we give him food."

Roadie opined, "A cat and a lion the same? Sir, obviously that is nonsense. Look at the deer, a wild animal of size. There are no small deer, none that I have ever seen. When a deer is being birthed, the fawn that is born is already sizable and can already run."

Edgar replied, "I don't understand that either. The lion had teeth as long the legs on that thing." He pointed to Tat and held out two fingers to show the length. "The two big fangs were like this."

Martha said, "Edith, please take that cat out. He is disturbing our guest."

Edith said, "Tat is tied to the table."

Martha said, "Then untie him. Get him out of here." Edith picked Tat up, untied him, and carried him outside. As she walked, she was stopped by Edgar, who held his two fingers out again to compare the size to Tat's leg.

"The fangs of the lion were *longer* than the legs of this animal," Edgar said. He gave a disapproving glance at Tat and shook his head. Then he said, "A pitiful creature. But even this cat does have those two fangs on the top of its mouth like a lion, just a lot smaller." Edith walked quickly back to her spot on the floor.

One of the children spoke to Roadie, "Sir, when a dog gives birth to puppies or when a cat gives birth to kittens, the puppies and the kittens are quite small. Then they grow much bigger."

Roadie said, "So an animal can be born small and then grow much larger. Well, you may have an idea there."

Snakes

Turning to Edgar, Roadie said, "Sir, maybe you can tell the children about the snakes in the Holy Land. It's one of my favorites out of all your stories. And it's always good for a scare. Besides that, sir, you used the word *snake* to describe William the Conqueror and I am not sure that the children knew what you meant."

Edgar replied, "Oh, the snakes, those terrible things. I will never forget how startling snakes are when you see one. One of our men nearly died after being bitten by a snake. He suffered in pain for two days. Terrible. He had some luck. One of the men he was with knew to put his mouth over the bite and suck out as much of the poison as he could."

The children expressed surprise audibly. Andrew asked, "They sucked poison out of the bite?"

Edgar replied, "That's right. We prayed over and over for the man, and finally our Lord the Almighty took mercy upon him and started to heal him."

Edith walked around nervously. She asked, "What happened that the man almost died?"

Another child asked, "What are the snakes in the Holy Land like?"

Edgar replied, "What are snakes? Well, of course you have never seen a snake in Scotland." Edgar was going to continue, but William interrupted him.

"Oh, now, Edgar, we *do too* have snakes in Scotland."

Edgar was surprised: "You do? They told me that there were no snakes in Scotland. I thought it would be too cold for them here."

William said, "Well, it depends on who are the 'they' that told you that, Edgar. Maybe 'they' just wanted you to be surprised, or maybe 'they' just like to lie to other people. Some people lie when they don't think it will hurt. But we have snakes here. I saw one, oh, I think it was the summer before last."

Agnes added, "You said that was in the field just out by the road."

William said, "That's right. The snake was out in the sunlight. I thought, *Hey, I should kill that thing just so I can show it to all the family here, so that everybody will know what one looks like.* But before I was able to get something to hit the snake with, it had gone and was down a hole somewhere."

Edgar asked, "So it is that unusual to find a snake?"

William said, "That is the only time that I have seen a snake here in Scotland, *ever.* I have told our young ones here not to get near a snake, but it's hard to explain to them what a snake is because they have never seen one. Is that still right?" The children all nodded affirmatively.

Edgar said, "It appears that once again I have learned something. So if I see a snake here in Scotland, it's dangerous?"

William replied, "Right, the snakes are poisonous here. They are called adders."

Edgar said, "There are adders on the Continent that I have seen. They are poisonous. How big is the Scotland adder?"

William said, "Oh, the one I saw was not very big." He held his hands about two feet apart. "I think that is part of the reason we don't see them much, is that they are small and there are not very many of them. But we have talked to some people who killed one, and they could see that it was poisonous. They had heard of someone who was bitten and got sick from it."

Edward asked, "So what makes a snakebite poisonous?"

Edgar said, "When we killed snakes in the Holy Land, we cut them open. They have two teeth on the top of their mouth. At the end of those teeth is an opening where the poison can come out. So when the snake bites, the poison comes right out."

Edward said, "I still can't imagine putting my mouth over a snakebite. That seems so terrible."

Edgar said, “It is bad. The man who was bitten was bleeding quite a bit. But it is better to suck this blood and poison out of the wound.”

Several of the listeners expressed some shock. Edith audibly gasped. Martha expressed her horror by saying, “I can’t imagine anything like that.”

Andrus smiled. “It’s not near as bad as giving birth to a child. And you, Martha, had six of them.”

Edgar was puzzled by that. He asked Martha, “You have six children?”

Martha replied, “Our oldest girl is Mary, and she has married and moved to Glasgow. We had two more, but we lost them. They were both between John and Edward.”

Edgar responded kindly, “I am sorry to hear such a thing.”

William added, “Agnes and I also lost a little one.”

Edith looked at her mother: “I don’t remember, Mother.”

Agnes responded kindly, “I’m sure that you don’t remember our little boy Duncan, because you were so little then.”

Edgar said, “So you have also lost one? I am sorry to hear that. The times that we live in are so trying. These are things that happened before I moved back to Scotland, so I did not know.”

Roadie asked Martha, “Is there a doctor near to where you live?”

Martha responded, “Doctor? Doctor? You are certainly in a dream.”

There was a momentary silence before Edgar asked, “Roadie, why have you not told me about the snakes in Scotland?”

Roadie replied, “Well, sir, I may twist this around in my mouth to be able to say it, but I did not know that you did not know that there are snakes in Scotland. In fact, I have seen snakes here in Scotland on a few occasions. That is partly why I asked you to talk about the snakes in the Holy Land, because I find it so amazing when you teach about the Holy Land snakes. What you say is very interesting.”

Edgar responded, “Ah, yes, Roadie, you are right. I still have more to say about snakes. Let me show you this belt holder on my pants. This is snakeskin that we took from the Holy Land.” Edgar slowly stood up and showed a belt loop. He said, “Come touch my belt holder.” The children came forward and touched the snakeskin. Edgar explained, “I just have this as decoration. I can remember the snakes because I kept this skin from a snake we killed. This skin shows how big around the snake was, like that." He put the tip of one of his fingers and his thumb together to make a circle.

One of the children said, "This feels like a rope."

Edgar continued. "The snakes are like a rope. They are long and thin. When we killed one, we could touch it. And you are right: it feels like a rope. Also, it is round like a rope. Snakes get about this long." Edgar held his hands about three feet apart. "Well, I say that some snakes are even longer than this. Some of the snakes have poison in their bite. Not all snakes are poisonous. The snakes in the Holy Land that are poisonous are called vipers. Now, the man that I was telling about was bitten by a viper, this one right here." Edgar touched his snakeskin. "The snakebite made him very sick for two days."

Edward asked, "How did this happen?"

Edgar replied, "This is what happened. It was just after sunset when he saw a place that looked like a good place to rest on the sand for the night—if the fellow could move a few rocks out of the way. But the snake was under the rock. Once he moved the rock, the snake bit him. So what one of his companions did was to put his mouth over the snakebite and try to suck out the poison, and then spit it out." The children recoiled again.

Edith asked, "Where did the snake bite him? And it took two days for the man to be better?"

Edgar replied, "The snake bit him on the leg. It took him two days before we were sure he was going to live. His leg turned color and was so sore that it was a month before he could walk straight again. Months later, he told me that he still had pain, but at least he was walking straight. That was the last time I saw him. The people in the Holy Land told us that people do die from snakebite."

Edith asked, "Were there many snakes?"

Edgar replied, "No, there were not very many snakes, but when we did see one, it was very surprising. It was so startling that we couldn't help but feel fear. We are soldiers and are not supposed to fear, but the sight of a snake was startling."

Edward said, "I don't see how the snakes move."

Edgar explained, "The snakes move like worms in the ground do. They move their body and slide."

Edward asked, "The snakes would be very slow then, wouldn't they?"

Edgar answered, "No, the snakes are much bigger than worms and can move much faster. If a snake wants to strike at you, it only takes a blink of an eye." Edgar moved his hand and arm quickly.

Edward had one more question: "This is the skin from the snake that bit the man?"

Edgar smiled. "This is part of it right here." He again reached for his belt loop at his side. "This is one viper that was cut into pieces very quickly!" Edward smiled broadly. "Very promptly! That snake received his just reward."

Edith said, "Are there snakes outside? If there are, then I'm afraid to go outside."

William corrected her by saying, "Edith, don't be afraid to go outside. Like I said, I have been in Scotland all of my life and have seen only one snake. So don't concern yourself. And you will not see a snake today, as it is way too cold for them now. They will be in their holes, deep in the ground. You will not have a chance to see one until spring or summer, when it is warmer."

Edgar added, "The people in the Holy Land told us about the same thing, that they saw the snakes only during spring and summer when it was very hot. After that, the snakes would go into hiding."

William said, "When you say *hot,* oh my golly. The sun is very fierce in the Holy Land. Until you have been there, to Jerusalem in July, oh God Almighty, you cannot know how fierce the sun can be."

Edgar agreed, saying, "That is right. If you have never left Scotland, you have no thought as to how hot the sun can become."

John said, "If we can get our Holy Land pilgrimage arranged, then I would like to feel the fierce sun."

Edgar said, "Now let me tell you this: there is a lesson from the Bible that I learned about because of the snakes in the Holy Land. When Adam and Eve were in the garden, they were tempted by the Serpent, which is another name for a snake. So in the Bible the promise was made that the Serpent, or the snake, would become the Enemy of people. And this has happened. In people, there is a fear of snakes that is unexpected. This is why the appearance of a snake is so startling to people. People have a natural and yet an unusual fear of snakes that started with Adam and Eve. And there is another lesson. During His ministry, Jesus confronted the Jewish leaders and the Pharisees many times. The Pharisees would be dressed in ornate garments. Their clothing would be black, or might be colored in patterns, just as the skin of the vipers. Jesus called these Jews who argued against Him poisonous snakes. Now can you picture that? Jesus called out these Jewish leaders right to their faces—"You poisonous snakes, you brood of vipers"—and He pointed at them. The Jewish leaders would have been wearing some colored and patterned clothes, so that is why Jesus compared their appearance to poisonous vipers. And, of course, Jesus was also making a comparison to the poisonous teachings that came out of the mouths of the Pharisees. Jesus was telling the Pharisees plainly that their appearance and their teaching were both poisonous. Everyone who saw and heard Jesus confront the Pharisees would have been able to see both of these comparisons and would have understood exactly what He meant."

John asked, "So the Pharisees would have understood this as well?"

Edgar replied, "Oh, surely they would have. It was a very direct insult. But the Pharisees were so wrapped up in their own customs and traditions that the Savior realized that confronting them directly would be the only way that any of them would change and recognize Him."

Andrus said, "You have done very well, Edgar, trying to explain what a snake is to children who have never seen one. And having that snakeskin is a very good example."

John added, "Indeed, those lessons are very interesting."

Constance spoke next. "And you are right about another thing: that William the Conqueror was a snake too." Several people smiled and laughed softly.

Edgar smiled. "Yes, he certainly was a snake."

Constance said, "He took our country away from us."

Andrus added, "So, children, please don't call anyone a snake. When you say that, you are calling that person a very low form of life."

William wanted to challenge the children, so he said, "This spring, when it gets warmer outside, we will look for a snake. We will try to hunt one down so everyone can see it. Just don't get too close to it."

Sheep

Edgar asked, "Children, you have sheep here that you tend, isn't that right?"

Edith replied, "Yes, there are some in a pen up the hill."

Edgar said, "There is another lesson that I want to teach you. Let me tell you about the sheep in the Holy Land. To start with, the sheep there look different."

Margie asked, "The sheep are different? How can that be?"

Edgar said, "I recall that their heads were longer and they had longer ears."

William added, "I can scarcely remember that, but now that you say it, I seem to remember that too, that the sheep were different-looking. When you travel to other parts of the world, the animals are, I think, different, as the land and the weather changes."

Edgar said, "Not only do the sheep in the Holy Land look different, but also they even behave differently than the sheep here in Scotland do. I developed this belief once I had observed them." Looking at the children, he asked, "What happens when you try to catch one of your sheep?"

Margie replied, "Well, we call them and sometimes they come, but usually they don't come, so we have them within a fence and we have to catch them."

Edgar said, "That's right, you have to catch them. And why is that?"

Edward answered, "It's because they don't want to be sheared."

Edgar said, "I don't believe the sheep have much anger about being sheared. I think that it is because here in Scotland there is green grass and plants and forage all over, so the sheep have no trouble at all finding food. If you approach them, they scatter. But in the Holy Land, the sheep are different; they have learned to behave differently. In the Holy Land, the sheep actually follow their shepherd. You see, there the land is not all green. There are many rocky places, sandy places, and patches of dry dirt where nothing is growing. So what happens? When the shepherd calls his sheep, or whistles at them, they follow him. And why do they follow him? Because the sheep know that the shepherd will lead them to food. The sheep know that they must not run off anywhere. They depend on their shepherd to lead them to green pastures. Now in the Bible, do you know what it says? 'The Lord is my shepherd. I shall not want, for he leads me to green pastures.' And what does Jesus say? He describes a shepherd who calls his sheep by name and leads them out. The sheep follow the shepherd. A stranger is someone the sheep will not follow. Jesus said, 'I am the Good Shepherd. My sheep know My voice and follow Me.' Whom is the Savior talking about now? Why, it is us. It is we who are following Jesus, of course."

John asked, "So, what you are saying is that the Bible is telling a different story?"

Edgar replied, "The Bible was written in the Holy Land, so it has to be understood in the context of life in the Holy Land. When our weather, our animals, and even our story about the snakes is, as you see, different from that of the Holy Land, then we may find it difficult to understand what the Bible is really teaching. This is why a pilgrimage to the Holy Land would be very helpful to all of you, if you can possibly go. And because the sheep here in Scotland are different and have such an easy life compared to sheep in the Holy Land, and because we scarcely need to tend to them at all, we are less able to understand the comparisons made to sheep in the Bible."

Andrus commented, "You know, Edgar, I never thought about that before, but you may be right. Looking back at it, I can see the how sheep in the Holy Land might behave differently."

Martha said, "I do all the sheep shearing for us, so if there is any way to make catching the sheep any easier, I would be all for that."

Andrus said, "Shearing is not usually a problem. Catching the sheep is the problem."

Edith said, "I want to see some sheep from the Holy Land. Could you bring some sheep from the Holy Land here?" That question brought some laughter from everyone.

Andrus said, "That would be a huge job for somebody. I don't think people will ever move animals very far, unless the animals are horses to ride."

John asked, "What about the story that Jesus tells of the ninety-nine sheep and the one that is lost?"

Edgar replied, "Another good picture. Imagine that you are a sheep. If you are in the Holy Land, you will say to yourself, 'I had better follow that two-legged fellow, the one who whistles and waves at me, so I can find food and water. That two-legged fellow knows just where to go. And if I get lost, I will be glad when the shepherd finds me and takes me back to the herd. Then I will have food and water again.' But what happens here in Scotland? If a sheep gets out of the pen, it will run away. Dare I say this? Oh, dare I say that if your sheep gets loose, you may as well wave 'ba-ba' to the sheep." Edgar held up his right hand and gave a quick "bye-bye" waving motion to accompany "ba-ba," causing everyone to laugh. He then continued speaking. "The sheep will run wild because there is pasture and water everywhere. You will be very fortunate to lure it back to you, isn't that right?"

Martha said, "That's right. If a sheep gets out of his pen, you may never see him again."

Margie countered, "Beck would come back to me, because he is my friend. And he is going to need his wool cut too."

John commented, "I have never seen a sheep that wants to get his wool cut off. And, Edgar, I will have to reread the stories about sheep in the Bible and consider what you said."

Break

Martha said, "Our lunch is ready. John, can you say our blessing?"

John replied, "Of a certainty I can. Shall we all stand, please?" At this, all present in the little church stood obediently and clasped their hands with each other's. Everyone knew to close their eyes as well. John said, "To our almighty Lord and Father in heaven: We give you praise and thanks for our gathering today and the many things we have learned. Now please bless this food as we eat, and we do humbly thank You for it. In the name of the Father, the Son, and the Holy Spirit. Amen." After that, a meal was served and all spoke gladly to one another.

Endnotes

1 Archibald Wilberforce, *The Great Battles of All Nations,* vol. 1 (New York: P. F. Collier and Sons, 1899). See also Rick Sinclair, "Battle of Hastings, 1066" *History of Clan Sinclair,* accessed April 28, 2015, http://sinclair.quarterman.org/history/med/battleofhastings.html.

Edgar's Message

Edgar Begins His Speech

The people in the church were finishing their meal when Edgar slowly stood up, drew his sword, and then tapped the sword on the table loudly enough to get everyone's attention. Edgar spoke. "I have a message that I want to share with you. One of the memories of my youth is of reading the Holy Scriptures. In the last few years, I have been able to return to reading the Scriptures once again. And as I am now older and have had many experiences in my life, I have found that the Scriptures are more true than I'd ever thought before. Now, I know that many of you are not used to sitting and listening to one man speak for a short time, but if I see anyone not listening then it's sska-put!" Edgar swept his sword through the air. Then his eyes twinkled and he let a small smile show as he pointed to Andrus and repeated, "Sska-put! Andrus smiled. Roadie stepped behind Edgar to reassure the audience that the former king was speaking in jest. Edgar slid his sword back into his scabbard. "I have to say once more that I am so filled with gratefulness and thanks to our Lord God Almighty, for He has spared my life so many times that I should live this long and be able to say that God has saved me. I can truly say that I am very thankful to be able to witness this moment.

"First, let me begin by remembering your father and grandfather, and even your great-grandfather Andreas. He is among the first men I remember. He came with us from Hungary, protecting us while we traveled. He served my family in the court of England and then in the court of Scotland. He fought for me through countless battles. And he could hunt and fish. Yes, he was very good at catching fish! And a skillful hunter. Of all the men I have ever known, Andreas was one of the most loyal and brave and faithful.

"So I will say this as a prayer to the memory of Andreas and as a dedication of this family church: O Almighty Father in heaven, I thank You for Your servant Andreas, and for allowing him to smile down on us even today."

Edgar's Testimony

Edgar continued his speech, saying, "As for me, let me say this: as I have grown older and older, I have spent as much time as the days allow to search the Scriptures and reflect on my life. I do this not because I want to reflect on my life, for that can become painful, but because helpful are the Scriptures for guidance and strength." Edgar turned to Roadie and asked, "Roadie, while we were riding in our carriage this morning, what were those words that you were trying to explain? *Regret* and, oh, what was it?"

Roadie replied, "Regret and remorse, sir."

Edgar said, "Ah, regret is when you remember what has happened, but remorse—tell me again?"

Roadie said, "Regret is remembering something unpleasant, something that you wish had not happened. Remorse is remembering something that you wish had not happened so much so that recalling it becomes a disturbance to your mind. The remorse becomes a wearisome mood covering your life."

Edgar replied, "Ah, well said, Roadie. Everyone will have a regret, something that they wish had not happened. There is regret for everyone; no one will escape regret. But remorse is the hurt of regret, the hurt that you continue to carry like a weight. And, Roadie, what does the remorse lead to?"

Roadie replied, "That's clear, sir. Men take to the heavy drink. That's what many men in my family do. They drink and then, in their folly of drunkenness, continue to relive their regrets. This is when the regret becomes remorse, such that that they will carry it as if they were holding a great and large stone. The remorse drains and drags away their life."

Edgar said, "Very well. Roadie and I have been talking about these things. I agree with what you have said, Roadie. I am surely fortunate to have a driver who can explain these words to me. Look at my life; I had a father who should have become king, but instead he was murdered. I became king, but I was pushed aside. I fought back and I was defeated. I tried to fight back and I was shipwrecked. I tried many times to regain the throne of England by using my friend Robert, but the obstacles were always too many. These are my regrets. And I have experienced remorse. The remorse pushes a man to destroy himself. But in the last few years, I have become able to understand what the plan of the Almighty has been for my life. I have fought for freedom, from the Holy Land all the way to Scotland, and now I am finally beginning to understand freedom. I have freedom, and I have pushed away the remorse." Edgar paused to make a pushing motion with his hands. "I have no remorse because of what the Almighty has done for me. My best memories are of the times when I prayed and God answered my prayer. The time our ship was lost in a storm at sea, the times I was in battle and feared for my life, the times we were camped and had no food, those are the times when my prayer was in truth, when it was a prayer for my life. There were prayers that I said as a child; these I no longer remember. The times that you pray as if your life depends on your prayer—these are the prayers that you will remember. My worst memories come when I recall the names and the faces and the voices of those who fell in battle while fighting for my cause." Edgar paused and looked heavenward. "This is when I was a young man. I felt the weight of those who were lost. I was overwhelmed by my failures. I had no belief. I attempted to study the Scriptures, but it appeared as if I could find nothing in them. I was a young man who had lost whatever I had learned in the church. This was a time when I prayed as if to search for God. I was looking for something to believe, and that wasn't going to be just what I heard in Mass at church. I searched the Scriptures for anything that I could understand, but there was nothing. I asked my friends, 'Do you have faith?' and "What do you believe?' They said, 'Of course.' I said, 'Is there even a God?' They replied, 'Of course; just believe it.' A glib answer, I thought. With a great sadness, I went away to my own camp; and then I suddenly felt the weight of God throughout my body. It was like a light throughout me. I felt something that I had never felt before, nor have I felt it since. It was a feeling all throughout my body and mind. I lay down across my bed and looked up. I was scarcely aware of my camp anymore. Then I could see the word *faith* as if written, and I could see the names God, Jesus Christ, and the Holy Spirit, and the word *Bible.* I could see my whole life disappearing into the word *faith,* and then, right away, I knew that I was a Christian. I had a new reason. I knew that I had to have faith in God, Jesus Christ, the Holy Spirit, and the Bible above all else. I now knew certainly that I was destined for heaven and had avoided the fire of hell. Ever since then, I have never doubted that He exists and that He is real, and that I am in the plan of the Almighty." Edgar looked toward his audience before continuing. "The very next day, I opened the Bible and starting reading. Suddenly, I understood what it said! I read about being born again, and now I knew that I was born again! I read about being filled with the Holy Spirit; and that had happened to me! The fires of hell had been close to me, but now they were gone! Heaven was close to me! I read about faith and grace and mercy; and now it was as clear as a window to me!"

Edgar looked toward John and said, "Now, John, you are studying for the priesthood. It is very well to say the Mass every day, but even just one time to gain the presence of the almighty God is worth far more than all the Masses you could ever say."

John responded, "I have felt His calling, sir."

Edgar said, "Very well. I desire that all of you find the presence of God, even if only one time. Some people want to say that they believe in God. That is well enough. For me, I now can discern the difference between faith and belief. My faith is in God, Jesus Christ, the Holy Spirit, and the Bible. Now when I say that I believe something, it might be something that may not happen. When Roadie drives our carriage home, I believe that he will get me home, but the wheel of our carriage may hit a rock in the road and we may suddenly find our carriage overturned in a gulley. I believe that we will get home, but we may find that the river has flooded and we cannot get across. I believe that we will get home, but rocks may have crashed down from a hill and blocked the road. I believe that we will get home, but, God forbid, we may be overtaken by robbers. And when we get home, what will we find? I believe that my friends and family will be there, but someone may have left, or maybe the house has been damaged by a storm or destroyed by a fire, or, God evermore forbid, someone had suddenly taken sick and is gone. This is the way that I think, such that I can divide faith from belief." Edgar took a paper from his coat pocket. "This is a Scripture: 'For ye are all the children of God by faith in Christ Jesus' [Galatians 3:26].* "And here is a Scripture in which I have found great meaning: 'But without faith it is impossible to please him: for he that cometh to God must believe that he is, and that he is a rewarder of them that diligently seek him' [Hebrews 11:6]. What a joy filled my heart when I realized that I now possessed faith! Faith was now something that I could touch! I now pleased God! The existence of God is now not in doubt for me, not even for one moment. I diligently sought God. It was very difficult to look for what I did not know, or whom I did not know. But then He rewarded me! He took me into His presence!"

John raised his arm to get Edgar's attention. "Sir, can you tell me where you found those Scriptures?"

Edgar replied, "Yes, I noted the first Scripture as being found in the Galatians book. The second Scripture about faith is near the end of the Hebrews book in the New Testament."

John replied, "Thank you, sir."

Edgar Teaches about Freedom

Edgar resumed speaking. "Let me say more about the verse found in Hebrews. Start at the end of the verse: I became diligent to seek Him. Seeking Him is difficult. Seeking Him requires study of the Scriptures and prayer. I sought Him diligently, but I did not know even for what or for whom I was searching. You look for Him everywhere and in everything, for you do not know where you will first find Him, or even when the Almighty shall reveal Himself. I sought Him diligently. But

---

* All scripture references used will be from the King James version of the Bible. In 1124, the King James Version of the Bible was still several centuries away from being published, but Edgar would be speaking something similar to old English.

I did not find Him. It was God who found me and rewarded me with joy. The next part of the Scripture is the middle: I came to Him first being convinced that He existed. I had to truly believe that He existed before I could really know for sure that He exists. I took a step to believe that He existed, and now the experience I had leaves me without doubt that He exists. Finally, consider the first part of the verse: the faith that I have is not my own; rather, it is faith that God gave to me. Just as I described a moment ago, I found my life disappearing into faith. Now I know that I please God! That is where the joy comes from! But as you see, every step through this Scripture is listed in order from the last to the first. First, I sought Him, and then He revealed Himself to me. Second, I believed that He existed, then I knew that He existed because He placed His hand on me. Last, I had faith, but it was the faith that He had given me. So when I found faith, I found that the Almighty Himself had brought me through every step. Every step through the journey of faith is His!"

Edgar pointed to the sky. "We know that the Scriptures give us some rules to live by and to use for purposes of governing ourselves. One example of this type of Scripture is the Ten Commandments. But there are many other stories and lessons in the Bible as well. I am most fortunate, for I was taught in the court of the king of England when I was just a lad. I was able to read many Bible stories. But then I became a man who experienced a lifetime of battles and grief and sorrow. Now I am older and I am able once again to read the Scriptures. With a lifetime of experiences and the guidance of the Spirit of God, I now understand some of the wisdom contained on those pages of the Holy Scriptures."

Edgar lowered his hand to his side and continued. "What I want to do is to give you as much hope and as much faith as I possibly can leave with you. And this is what I have been doing: traveling to as many of our friends as possible to start and encourage family churches around here near Edinburgh. In the past few years, I have been able to help several churches get started. And even if the church appears to be just at the beginning stages of being built in a very new and informal building, as looks to be the case here, I am still pleased and proud to be a part of starting the growth of the church. So to give you this hope, I am going to talk about freedom. It is an idea that is very hard to understand, the idea of freedom is.

"If we mount a horse and we set off to ride, we become free to move wherever the horse is able to tread. Another way to explain freedom is to use a boat as a comparison. As soon as leave the shore, we are free to sail about in any direction we want to go. If we can walk, tend our fields and livestock, and own our land and house, then we are free.

"The opposite of freedom is slavery. Everyone is subject to the king, for instance. If the king decides to compel you to pay a tax, then you must pay a bit for your freedom. If the king decides that you must be grouped in his army or into his servitude, then you have your freedom to move about taken away. You have to move at the orders of the king. But the worst would happen if an invading army came and took you as a slave or even killed you. Then your freedom would be gone. Do you understand this?

"But there are ideas about freedom in Scripture. And when I saw these, I suddenly saw the conviction of what had directed the path of my entire life, and the truth of this conviction. Suddenly I realized that I had used my entire life to fight for freedom! Each and every battle I ever fought was to get freedom, whether for England or for Scotland or for France or even for the Holy Land. I had not even realized that I was being pushed along by the purpose of freedom." Edgar looked again to his paper with written notes on it. "I have found several verses of Scripture that speak to the idea of freedom. Let me read this to you: 'Stand fast therefore in the liberty wherewith Christ hath made us free, and be not entangled again with the yoke of bondage' [Galatians 5:1]. There is another one: 'There is neither Jew nor Greek, there is neither bond nor free, there is neither male nor female: for ye are all one in Christ Jesus' [Galatians 3:28]. This means we are all free in Christ. Indeed, even our Lord Jesus says this: 'If ye continue in my word, then are ye my disciples indeed; And ye shall know the truth, and the truth shall make you free' [John 8:31–32]. The idea of freedom." Edgar permitted himself to have just a momentary smile. "And I can see by looking into your faces and eyes that you have never considered this. Let me try to explain this idea, for I have found this to be important for every direction we set for ourselves."

At this point, John interrupted Edgar by saying, "Sir, may I ask where I could find the Scriptures that you have read?"

Edgar replied, "The Scripture where Jesus is speaking is in the gospel of John. You will find that easy to remember."

John said, "Yes, I know right where to find that one Scripture. I know the gospel of John rather well. And the other verses are where?"

Edgar answered, "The other two Scriptures are in the Galatians book. I realize Scriptures can always be difficult to find when you are trying to find a certain one. But Galatians is not very long. Here, take these." Edgar then gave John the paper with the Scriptures' chapters and verses written on it.

John replied, "Thank you, sir."

Edgar said, "Certainly, John. I'll leave you with each of my papers as I finish. What I want you all to consider is this: freedom for the church, freedom for the individual, freedom for the family, and freedom for Scotland. I want you to keep these important ideas at the front of your thinking. Indeed, let us all say these. Repeat what I say. Freedom for each person." Edgar waited for those gathered to repeat the saying. Once they did, he found that it was rather weak. Edgar said to the group, "Let's try that again: freedom for each person!"

This time, those gathered understood. They responded, "Freedom for each person."

Edgar said, "Better! Now repeat this: freedom for each family!"

The group managed a better response—"Freedom for each family!"

Edgar said, "A bit better. Now, freedom for Scotland!"

This utterance made the people more enthusiastic. They responded loudly, "Freedom for Scotland!"

Feudalism

Edgar started to speak again. "Now let me show you what is happening in England and Europe. I need seven people to show this. I need seven people from the family to line up right here. Let's take the children and three adults." Edgar picked the four children and then chose John, Agnes, and Martha. "Perfect," he said. He pointed at some of the children and told them, "Line up in order, from shortest to the tallest. All you have to do is kneel. If you can't kneel, then we will find someone who is willing and able."

As the line stretched out, Tat the house cat was found to be in the way of the line formation. Martha ordered, "Edith, take Tat outside." Edith took Tat and placed him outside. She then quickly rejoined the line. The family found their places. Edith, the youngest girl, was shortest and first in line. Margie was second, Edward was third, and Andrew was fourth. Agnes was shorter than Martha, so they lined up fifth and sixth, respectively. John, the tallest among them, took his place last in line. With a mixture of children and adults, there was a noticeable contrast in height.

Edgar admired the line. "Now, this line from the shortest to the tallest is just to give you a picture. It does not mean anything about children or adults. Instead, I intend to illustrate the placement of people in our society. What I would like to do now is to demonstrate how freedom is being taken away from the people of England and Europe."

Edgar walked to stand behind Edith. "The least important in the line is the peasant. A person of this status may also be called a serf. The peasant will be trusted with only the most elementary jobs. The peasant does all the hardest work. Peasants sow the seeds, plow the ground, and reap the crops. They thresh the seeds from the straw and make hay for feed and for thatch." Edgar stepped over to Margie. "The next person in line is the servant. Now the peasant must kneel and face the servant, and the servant faces the peasant. The peasant places her hands in the hands of the servant and gives an oath of loyalty." Edgar made sure that Edith knelt down and placed her hands in the hands of Margie. "There. The peasant has given her oath of loyalty. Edith, you must remain kneeling." Edgar now began to speak about Margie. "The servant does all the cooking and the cleaning. Servants take care of all the work within the house."

Edgar next moved to Edward. "The next person is the yeoman. Margie, you must now kneel and face the yeoman, and the yeoman must face the servant. You have to place your hands in the hands of the yeoman and give an oath of loyalty." Edgar looked back to Margie. Margie obediently knelt down to face Edward. When she touched her hands to Edward's, Edgar smiled and said, "Very good. Now you are loyal." Looking to Edward, Edgar said, "The yeoman is an attendant in a noble house and will do errands for the nobles." Edgar moved to Andrew. "The next in line is the freeman. But whether or not he is really free, certainly that is open to question. Edward, you must now kneel and place your hands in the hands of the freeman. Andrew, you must face the yeoman." Edward obediently knelt down and faced Andrew. When the two touched hands, Edgar proclaimed, "There, very loyal." Edgar stepped next to Agnes. "The freeman will farm his own land, or he may have a craft such as blacksmithing, but he also must give an oath of loyalty. Agnes, you are the knight, the first female knight." This drew a laugh from everyone, as it seemed very improbable to have a lady knight. "Andrew, you must face the knight, and kneel and give your oath of loyalty. And, knight, you must receive the oath from the freeman." Once again, Edgar made sure that Andrew knelt, faced Agnes, and placed his hands in her hands. When this step was completed, Edgar announced, "Wonderful. Extremely loyal." Edgar began to describe the knight by placing his hand on Agnes's shoulder. "A knight is the man whom I most admire, of course, because the knight is the fighting man. He is trained and skilled in the use of all weapons: the two-handed sword, the battle-ax, the lance, the dagger, and the mace. The knight is skilled in horsemanship and has trained his horse to ride as a part of himself. The knight is courageous, devout in faith, and chivalrous." Edgar moved to Martha. He said, "The next person in line is the nobleman. Agnes, you must now kneel and face the noble. Nobleman, you must face the knight. Place your hands in the hands of the noble to give your pledge of loyalty." Agnes and Martha obeyed the command. Edgar continued. "That's the stuff. Excellent loyalty, Agnes.

"Andrus, William, come here. I want you to watch this carefully so that I can hear your comments. Now let me tell you how to become a knight." Andrus and William stood and walked over to stand near Agnes and Edgar. Edgar then continued: "A boy from seven to fourteen years of age in training to become a knight is called a page. Next, the young man who is between fourteen and twenty-one years of age is called a squire." The effect of these statements caused disapproving expressions on the faces of Andrus and William. Edgar continued.

"When the young man has completed all of his training and is ready to become a knight, the nobleman will 'dub' the knight by touching the squire as he kneels. Using the back of his hands, he touches each of the new knight's shoulders. Since you are Agnes, you will be known as Sir Agnes. Now, Martha, you can touch Agnes on the shoulders and say, 'I dub thee Sir Agnes.' Edgar assisted Martha with moving her hands as she accomplished this simple task. "Very well done, Martha. This is like a game, is it not?" Again, this caused some derisive laughter in the crowd.

William shook his head. "Around here, nobody is going to call me 'sir.'"

Edgar looked toward William and Andrus. He said, "But this is what they are doing now in England and Europe. William and Andrus, you are two of the best knights I have ever led into fighting, but I know that your training was not nearly as severe as the training undergone by young men today. People are taking a boy of just seven years of age and are committing his life for him while he is still a boy."

Andrus said, "That is cruel. You don't need to start training a boy to become a knight when he is a child of seven. A young one like that is just starting to do some gardening and learn some craft. We thought John would be a knight when he was little, but now he is devoted to the priesthood."

William also responded to Edgar, saying, "There are some tricks to fighting to be learned, but it shouldn't take that much training to learn how to swing a sword or bash your opponent with a mace. A young boy can learn some things about fighting just by playing."

Andrus added, "We did not have to do all that training and we were just fine."

Edgar said, "I know for certain that you two were the bravest of knights. You know well of what you speak. Now, back to our line." Edgar stepped back to his place next to Martha while Andrus and William returned to their chairs. Edgar said, "The nobles act as owners and handle the finances of the land. They collect rent and pay taxes. They give orders to all the peasants and the servants, and the former act as judges over the latter, even giving them permission to marry. If the kingdom is facing conflict, the nobles will arrange for the knights and the other men to assemble for the military." Edgar smiled as he became sarcastic. "There are more titles for nobles than I can shake a stick at. You have barons, you have earls, you have dukes, you have lords. And I know that there are many others."

Edgar came to stand behind John. "Finally, we reach the king. The king commands the entire state. His contact with the kings and nobles of nearby states is to ensure that peace is maintained. Should the threat of war come, the king must call on his nobles and knights to assemble all of their fighting forces, including the yeomen and the freemen who are prepared for service. The king collects a tax from the nobles and thus accumulates wealth. The king will determine who should become new noblemen, where their land should be located, and what the boundaries of their land should be. So now, Martha, you are the nobleman and you must kneel before the king, placing your hands in his and making your oath of loyalty." Martha then knelt before John and placed her hands in his. When this was completed, Edgar motioned with his arm all the way down the line and said, "There, perfect loyalty all the way!" Then Edgar stood to the side and looked toward the line. Seeing John standing and the other six people still kneeling, he moved his arm to point at them. He thundered, "Look at this! Do you see freedom here? Or is this a picture of the miserable human condition?" After a pause, Edgar spoke to those in the line: "You may stop kneeling now. Go and return to where you were seated. Your performance was perfect. But, John, you must stay by me for another moment. I am not finished with you yet."

The six who had been kneeling now rose and returned to their chairs. Edgar held John's arm. "But, John, you thought that when someone was a king, nothing bad could happen to him, but that is not so. As I told you before, when you are a king, everyone is trying to kill you, so you never know when even one of your subjects may press the dagger in your back or persuade you to sip of the cup that has been poisoned. But that is not all. A different king with a fighting force from a nearby country may come and take your kingdom. What should you do then? You may have to kneel in front of that other king and plead for your life. If you find any favor with that king, then he may allow you to remain as a noble, but you will then have to make your oath of loyalty to him." Edgar released John from his grip. "John, of course you know that the church has its own order. I know that it starts with the monk. Now tell us the rest."

John said, "That is quite correct, sir. A man starts as a monk, which is what I am now, and a woman will become a nun. From monk, a man becomes a dean, then a prior, then an abbot, and then an archdeacon. The next steps are the big ones, when you reach archbishop, then bishop, and finally pope."

Edgar responded, "That is correct, John. As you see, the church has even one more step, making a total of eight steps. And every king is subject to the pope. John, you may return to your seat." John returned to his chair. Edgar moved to the center of the room. "Now, in the church, I can see that as you gain knowledge and experience, you can move to a higher step. And as craftsmen or knights, you must attain a level of training. But I can see no freedom in these steps that people are being forced to follow. I have decided that if the Devil himself were to organize humanity, this is exactly what he would design. For every man is flawed, and every man will not be able to live by his oath of loyalty. Even worse, every man is capable of being deceptive and betraying another. There can be nothing worse than a person being forced to work for another person, and that person being forced to work for another person, and that person being forced to work for yet another, all the way up the line. So do you see what I am saying? This has to be the plan of the Devil himself."

Freedom for Scotland

Edgar continued speaking. "The first freedom that we must concern ourselves with is the freedom of our country of Scotland. We must never let ourselves be enslaved by the English or the Vikings or the Normans or any other power. When a foreign power invades another country, it is because the king of the invading country desires to exert his power and extract the wealth. This is exactly what William the Conqueror would say." Mimicking a French accent, Edgar said mockingly, "Exert the power and extract the wealth." He returned to his usual speaking voice and said, "When a country has the order that I have just demonstrated to you, the natural desire of the king is going to be to exert power and take wealth. Royals have no concern for people, for they consider that people are peasants, serfs, and servants. This is a grave concern for us, as the kingdoms throughout the world are always established so that the king may become wealthier. England did not have this social structure when I was a boy. England then had the same culture of freedom that we enjoy in Scotland right now. England had this structure forced upon them by the Normans. I fought against the Normans as long as I could. I fought to try to rid England of this oppression. I have even fought to free the Holy Land. So you see that I have spent my entire life fighting for freedom."

Freedom of the Church

Edgar once again looked at his written notes and began reading: "We must keep our church free. These are the words of the Savior Jesus: 'If ye continue in my word, then are ye my disciples indeed. And ye shall know the truth, and the truth shall make you free' [John 8:31–32]. This is in the gospel of John." Edgar gave these notes to John before resuming. "Jesus faced the persecution of the Jewish religious leaders. Then, when the Christian church first started, there was great persecution from the Jews and the Romans. Many of the early Christians became martyrs for the faith. There are still places in the world where a Christian will be martyred, just as some of my friends were martyred in the Holy Land. The church will grow as we meet the challenges of life and death. Remember this: the church is made to meet the challenges of life and death. But the church and the people of the church must be free. The church can be crushed into the ground just the same as a country can be crushed by an invader. But even if these events occur, God will save people. People will choose freedom and choose Christ."

Edgar looked toward William and Andrus and asked, "Men, when you receive a message, what do you do with it?"

There was a pause, then William asked, "What are you trying to ask?"

Edgar said, "Someone has brought news. What do you think when you receive a message of news?"

Andrus replied, "I think that I have to understand what the news is about."

Edgar said, "You begin to make a judgment of the news. Is the news true, or is it a lie? Is the news truthful, or has something happened after the messenger has left? A message can be truthful, can be wrong, or can be a lie. There are more chances that the message you received is a deception rather than a factual account. Pray that you will always have a truthful messenger. And begin to weigh the news to see if you can determine the worth of what you have heard. But I have seen men who read the Holy Bible and then try to decide if the Bible is correct. This is a great folly. The Bible is the message of God and is to be regarded as truth. While a messenger can bring news that may be right or wrong, you must never pronounce judgment on God's Word. This is like making a judgment of God, when it is God who will judge us. Men who have tried to judge Scripture fall into a mass of confusion in their minds."

Freedom in Your Family

Edgar said, "Your family and the people you live with and work with must be kept free of sin. Everyone is to avoid sin. You must love your brother, your sister, your parents.

"As I am old now, I have been enjoying reading the Scriptures. What else would I want to do? I can no longer fight or work very much. And how astonishing are the stories of King Saul, King David, King Solomon, and the other kings of Israel. It is just like this very day, a kingdom and a family that is full of treachery!

"Now I will look at my notes carefully." (Edgar once again took a paper from his pocket.) "I was recently reading the story of King David over and over. Do you remember the story of David and Bathsheba?" Several people nodded yes. "Ah, but let me ask you some more questions. First, do you remember the name of Bathsheba's husband? And what was the name of the prophet who came to confront David in his sin? Now let me tell you.

"As I mentioned, I had been reading the story of David and Bathsheba again and again; just something about that story lifted my interest. It must be that I have seen this treachery time and again in castles and kingdoms all around Europe. When Bathsheba is introduced in the Scriptures, she is named as the wife of Uriah the Hittite. I suppose a few days later, as I continued to read, I found a list of men who were close to King David. We would consider them to be knights today. These men were listed as David's palace guards. So as I was reaching the end of this list of names, I found that the very last name on the list was of Uriah the Hittite. I had read this before many times but had paid no attention to it. But this time, I saw it, and my thought was simply a question: have I not seen that name before? I continued my reading, searching back and forth through that section of the Scriptures. I decided to mark the place in the Scriptures to see if I could find the other place where I had seen the name of Uriah the Hittite. Finally I found it after many days of searching. Indeed, when Bathsheba is introduced, she is identified as the wife of Uriah the Hittite. So when David took Bathsheba, he was not taking someone who was unknown to him. In an act of sin and treachery, David stole the wife of one of his palace guards! But, just wait, I found more! I will tell you about two other names that I found. Also listed as one of David's palace guards is Eliam the son of Arithophel. When Bathsheba is introduced, she is also identified as the daughter of Eliam. And Arithophel, who is listed as an adviser to David, is also mentioned several other places in the story. This, then, is David's sin: he stole Bathsheba, who was the wife of Uriah and the daughter of Eliam, who were both among David's palace guards—and Bathsheba was the granddaughter of one of David's closest advisers. I am certain that David had known of Bathsheba when she was but a small girl, even an infant. David had been keeping his eye on Bathsheba and considering engaging in sin with her for a long time [from 2 Samuel chapters 11–12, 23].

"We know that David arranged a way for Uriah to be killed in battle. And after David's sin came to be known, Arithophel betrayed David. Because it is so dreadful, I shall not even mention what happened to Arithophel afterwards.

"But the Lord noticed David's sin and appointed a prophet to come to David. Now, who was the prophet that came to David? Does anyone know? It was Nathan the prophet who came to confront David with his sin. Nathan the prophet confronted David by telling a story that tricked David into condemning himself. Then I saw this: Nathan told David that as a result of his deeds, a sword would be held over his family. Let me show you!" Edgar withdrew his sword from his scabbard and held it straight in the air over his head.

A sword will be held over the house of David. This sword will never depart from your house! *Westbow Press Illustration*

Edgar first spoke to explain the sword. "This story is actually why I brought this sword today, so that I could show you this picture. Now Nathan told David, 'A sword will be held over the house of David! This sword will never depart from your house!' What does that mean? First, Nathan told David plainly that as the result of the latter's sin, the child that would be born to Bathsheba would die. Then Nathan promised that calamity would come to the house of David, and this would bring great embarrassment to David. The kingdom that David established would eventually be taken from his family. This downfall started when David's son Absalom murdered another son of David named Amnon. Eventually, Absalom was also killed, which caused David great grief. After David died, his son Solomon became king. Even though Solomon was considered to be the wisest of all men who ever lived, eventually sin overcame Solomon. When Solomon died, the kingdom split into two kingdoms, Israel and Judah. Eventually, both of these kingdoms fall. Thus, the sin of David against Bathsheba is the beginning of the scattering of David's family and of the downfall of David's kingdom. Both David and Solomon reigned forty years, so the time span from David and Bathsheba to the death of Solomon and the split of the kingdom is, it appears, about eighty years." Edgar put his sword back into his scabbard and spoke again. "I am going to say that I may be the only man in history who will ever notice these relations between the people identified in this story. But of all the men who ever lived, I have experienced and seen more treachery than most will ever see, which makes me the very best at finding the treachery. I think that is why I have read these stories so many times!"

The End of the House of Wessex

Edgar continued speaking to the family. "Now let me make a comparison of the House of David and my house, the House of Wessex. The House of Wessex was established about the year 500 with the legendary King Arthur. Since then, for hundreds of years, the history of the House of Wessex has been long and glorious. However, in about 987, King Edward was murdered by another member of the family who was jealous and who thought that another man, Aethelred, who is my great-grandfather, should be elevated to king. Now if you have learned this history, you will know that this was Edward the Martyr. As he was

Aethelred's half-brother, Edward the Martyr is my uncle going back just three generations before me. You have heard of the many miracles that followed his death. Indeed, Edward has been accorded the status of a saint in the church. At the time of Edward's assassination, a godly man prophesied great trouble ahead for England. And this has certainly come to pass; the prophecy has been fulfilled. For soon after Edward's murder, the Vikings invaded England and almost ended the House of Wessex. I am alive only because my father was sent into exile, where he lived almost all his life. Now I am old, and when I am gone the House of Wessex is ended. And as you will understand, from 987 to 1066 is seventy-nine years, just about the same length of time as the fall of the House of David and Solomon. Because of this, I have made this decision: that I will have no monument to myself, nor any gravestone. I strictly order you that you do not provide any such monument in my honor. Thank you for your offer to etch my name in stone on the church wall, but please do not do such a thing. I want no marker or memorial anywhere. Indeed, I have ordered Roadie and my other friends to place no marker in my place at all, for I am unworthy of even a gravestone. When I should pass, which at my age may happen soon, my friends shall simply place me on a boat, sail a short ways out to sea, and lay me overboard. This way, the fish and the creatures in the sea will finish me such that there will be no need to ever inter my remains. Why, even the remains of John the Baptist and many of the apostles are gone. We do not know where they may exist. I am the last of the Royal House of Wessex. No family member will remember me. Is it not the truth that the evil and wicked leaders of this world have statues and gravestones while the righteous vanish into the earth? Include me with the righteous! Now, you might ask how I can compare the House of David to the House of Wessex. The lesson is this: you must make sure that you keep your family and yourselves free from sin. The sin that you commit now will become like a wave on the ocean that is aroused by a fierce storm and breaks over whatever it touches."

The Example of Paul

Edgar paused, put down his paper, and took another paper from his pocket. He said, "What do you suggest? That I should feel at a loss for my entire life? Let me read what the apostle Paul wrote." Edgar read 2 Corinthians 11:24–27.

> Of the Jews five times I received forty lashes save one. Thrice I was beaten with rods, once I was stoned, thrice I suffered shipwreck, a night and a day I have been in the deep [sea]; In journeyings often, in perils of waters, in perils of robbers, in perils by mine own countrymen, in perils by the heathen, in perils in the city, in perils in the wilderness, in perils in the sea, in perils among false brethren; in weariness and painfulness, in watchings often, in hunger and thirst, in fastings often, in cold and nakedness.

"And after that, do you know what he wrote?" Edgar added 2 Corinthians 12:7–10.

> There was given to me a thorn in the flesh, the messenger of Satan to buffet me, lest I should be exalted above measure. For this thing I besought the Lord thrice, that it might depart from me. And he said unto me, My grace is sufficient for thee: for my strength is made perfect in weakness. Most gladly therefore will I rather glory in my infirmities, that the power of Christ may rest upon me. Therefore I take pleasure in infirmities, in reproaches, in necessities, in persecutions, in distresses for Christ's sake: for when I am weak, then I am strong.

Edgar asked, "Do you know why I have studied these Scriptures?" He paused. "Look at the incredible example set by Paul! For I was in danger sometimes in battle, but Paul was in constant danger. And I was once captured and was fortunate to be treated kindly, but Paul must have been captured at least nine times to have been flogged so many times. And my sister Margaret's boat was wrecked, and my ship was wrecked, but Paul said he was shipwrecked three times and survived a day in the sea! And then what else?! Paul is many times without food, water, and sleep. I have seldom had to do without; in fact, many times I have enjoyed the feasts of kings! And I can never say that I was cold and naked, because, in truth, I have often slept in castles!

"And then Paul had an injury that is unknown, but he was not deterred. He delighted himself in the insults and persecutions brought against him. In contrast, today we look for offenses so that we may have an excuse to attack our neighboring country and force them into a war! We also know that Paul was ultimately executed in Rome, and at a lesser age than my age right now. So if the great apostle is my example, then how should I regard my setbacks? Have I suffered? No! The great apostle is my inspiration. And now my mission to Scotland is just the same as Paul's mission. I can now see my life as a great blessing instead!" Edgar looked toward Roadie and said, "That is exactly the way we talked about saying this!"

Roadie replied, "Very well said, sir. I do know you personally, and I can see that this message comes from your heart. If you were trying to compare yourself to the apostle Paul, this might be … well … a bit weighty, sir."

Edgar replied, "We intend to speak to a large number of people so that my mission is just like the mission of the apostle. But I also know you would like me to remain humble."

Roadie replied, "My mission is to get you to our next stop before it gets dark. If we can leave here very soon, we can get there."

Edgar replied, "A very good idea, Roadie. Let me hurry along. I have one more idea for everyone here to consider."

The Return of Christ

Edgar's eyes twinkled as his next idea came into his mind. "This is another important idea. Children, friends, do you know that Christ has promised to return?" He looked carefully to the children and pointed to them as he smiled.

One of the children, Andrew, finally spoke up and said, "We say that in the creed that is spoken in Mass, correct?"

Edgar brightened even more. "You are right. But do you realize that this will be a real event, that history will be changed forever when Christ returns? Christ told the disciples several times that He would return. Then, after the resurrection, He appeared to the disciples and other people several times as well, so the people who lived in the first years after Christ was crucified were convinced that He would return to them very soon. But Christ did not return then. History has progressed for more than eleven hundred years since Christ was crucified. But now I have come to realize something that causes wonder and excitement even to me: that Christ is going to return a few short years from now! Tell me, children, what is the number of the year that is coming soon, a number with two simple digits?"

Andrew offered a reply. "Um, well, the next year is 1125."

Edgar sighed. "You are not quite understanding what I meant. Let me explain. The year that I'm thinking of is 1133! And it will be the year 1133 in just nine more years from now—in truth, just over eight years. All of us will, or at least most of us should, still be alive then. Do you recognize the numbers when I write 1133? The first two digits are ones, and two ones together make eleven. Then comes two digits of three. For thirty-three, you put two threes next to one another. So for the entire year 1133, you would write two ones followed by two threes. And that is I what I would consider to be very important about this particular year. For as I look at and study the pages of Scripture that I have, I see that numbers are part of understanding the Holy Writing. So look at what I see; the number one stands for God, and the number three stands for the Trinity. But there are two of each of the digits, so the year 1133 is a perfect double. Now this is important in the Scripture, because many concepts have two meanings. For example, Jesus told a man whom he was healing that his sins were forgiven. Christ did this to connect the two meanings with the same event. So the year 1133 is a very unique double set of digits. But now look at what else the year 1133 represents: exactly eleven hundred years past the event of the resurrection of Christ! After realizing this, I then realized what I had been a part of in the year 1100: it was the final success of our Crusade to retake Jerusalem and the Holy Land! The study of Scripture and our understanding is that Jerusalem would be returned to the hands of the believers just before He returned. When I realized all these things, I, I tell you, began shaking my fist in excitement. For, you see, now the meaning of my life came to me, that I could be a part of the preparation for His great return. Now I see the cause of all the setbacks and losses in my life: I have been a part of the plan of the Almighty. The battles I lost when I was young became lessons for the success of the battles of the Crusade!

"I now know through experience what my part in the plan of the almighty God is. Everyone has a part in the plan of the Almighty. And every one of you can find your place in that plan. You need to pray so that you discover that your place is important.

"So, you see, my place shall be at the very top of history. Obviously I will not be likened to William the Conqueror or to the Roman Caesars or to Alexander the Great or to any other of the evil and treacherous leaders. I will be compared to the righteous leaders, not to the evil leaders. I will be compared to Constantine, who led the conversion of Rome to Christianity. And would I be compared to John the Baptist, who prepared the way for our Lord? For if the Lord should return soon, I will have been one of the first who led the way. I will have pointed the way for the return of our Lord. And what should happen if Christ should not return in 1133 or does not return soon at all? It will not matter, for Jesus said Himself that He does not know the day of His return, but only the Father, the Almighty in heaven, knows the time of His return. What I have told you about the date of the approaching year is interesting and thought-provoking, but we must simply remain faithful as we watch and wait. We do not know. Why, we can scarcely imagine what the weather in Scotland will be like on the next day or even in the next hour. Roadie and I have talked about these things as we've studied together." Edgar looked toward Roadie and said, "I covered that in a short space of time, Roadie."

Roadie replied, "Again, very well said, sir. However, if you were trying to compare yourself to John the Baptist, once again, this might be … again, a bit weighty, sir."

Edgar replied, "And once again, you are always keeping me humble. But you will see."

Edgar's Rally

Edgar said to the group, "This has been my message. Now that you have heard my message, you must be sure to remember everything. Let's make this clear. Everyone, stand up! Everyone, all of you!" With everyone standing, Edgar began his rally. "Now repeat after me: Keep myself free from sin."

The family repeated in unison: "Keep myself free from sin."

Edgar then commanded the second oath: "Keep my family free from sin."

The family repeated in unison: "Keep my family free from sin."

Edgar then commanded the third oath: "Keep Scotland free!" He then repeated this so that everyone in the audience got the idea to repeat the three oaths. When everyone had completed saying the oath satisfactorily and loudly, Edgar concluded by saying, "That is what I wanted to hear. With your voices raised, you are like a powerful fighting force ready to go to battle. Allow me to say a prayer that is short and to the point." Edgar closed his eyes and clasped his hands together in front of his chest. He spoke slowly as he said, "Our Father, our Lord Jesus, let everyone here move forward in Your presence. Come to us, touch us, and help us see and feel You. Guide and direct each one of us as we do our part for Your kingdom. In the name of the Father, the Son, and the Holy Spirit. Amen." Then, with a motion of his arms, Edgar permitted the audience to sit once again.

Edgar Leaves

Roadie stepped toward Edgar and said, "Very well done, sir." Facing the church audience, Roadie said, "People of this church, as we have been traveling, Edgar has been giving this message to various churches. We want people to be united in faith and in common spirit throughout our country. And may I say today that you have seen and heard Edgar's best teaching session yet. But now I must make a finish to our day here, as we must make our next appointment. Now I can even see a bit of sunshine in between the clouds, so if Edgar and I can leave very soon, we can make it to our destination before it gets too dark to see."

Edgar said, "Thank you very much, Roadie. You always see what is ahead for me."

Andrus, the first to shake Edgar's hand, congratulated the former king. "This has been a wonderful message, Edgar. Our family will remember this for a long time."

John was the next to reach Edgar. "Thank you, sir. I have learned very much today from you. I can find all of the Scripture passages that you have mentioned. And I will write some notes that I will use as we begin our church." With that statement, John returned to Edgar his written notes.

William, Agnes, and Martha also gathered near Edgar. William spoke. "Edgar, your speech was incredible. It was wonderful. And this talk that we have had today has helped feel better. I think you are right about this, that talking about past events will help me release the memories that bother me."

Agnes added, "Thank you, Edgar. I think that you helped William today. I think he will feel better."

Martha said, "Your speech was wonderful. Freedom is going to come someday."

Andrus decided to make a statement about freedom. "I believe that what you are talking about when you talk about freedom is a value that we can strive to achieve."

Edgar answered, "That's very much right. In the England of my youth, we had a slight amount of freedom, but certainly there is a loss of freedom in England and Europe today, as I showed to you in that line."

Constance waved for Edgar to come close to her. When Edgar appeared beside her, she said, "Edgar, I remember when you were just a boy who was often afraid. You remember that, don't you?"

Edgar nodded. "Sure, if you say so."

Constance said, "You surely have come a long and have had a tough road through life. Your speech shows all the wisdom that you have gained. That was great, wonderful, everything good."

Edgar was prodded by Roadie, who said, "We must make sure to take this back." Constance had been holding the Holyrood. Edgar stepped to reach the Holyrood and slowly lifted it from Constance's lap.

Constance asked, "You mean I don't get to keep it?"

Edgar replied, "I am so sorry, dear, but I must." Holding the sacred object, he let each person in the room look at it one more time.

Andrus said, "Edgar, thank you for coming. This has been the most memorable Christmas Day ever." Others also nodded and offered their thanks.

Edward asked, "Will John now be able to say the Christmas Mass before you leave?"

Edgar replied, "That would be best, but we had better get going now. Roadie is watching out for me, so we must not let that sunlight get away."

John replied, "Maybe we can have Mass later. Edgar has spoken much more of a Mass than anything I can say right now. I think I shall try to write down some of the teachings he has given to us."

Edward and the other children stepped forward to get closer to Edgar. Edward said, "Sir, I hope that you can come back and tell us more."

Edgar touched each one of the children on their shoulder and replied, "I sure hope I can come back. Roadie, are we very busy?"

Roadie replied, "Sir, we travel every week to visit churches. And you want to visit every church in Scotland, which, of course, is not possible. Then, after we travel for a few days, you need to rest."

Edgar replied, "Roadie, we need to make a note that we will come back here soon, as we are not very far from Edinburgh." Edgar stood near Constance to let her see the Holyrood close up one more time before he closed the case.

Constance said, "Thank you very much, Edgar. Now I will be able to cross that great river to the other side."

Edgar said, "I am going to the other side of the mountain soon."

Constance asked, "Agnes, Martha, will you help me stand up?" Agnes came to one side, and Martha came to the opposite side, of Constance. The two slowly were able to help her to her feet. Constance put her finger on Edgar's chest and said, "Now I'm going to go to the other side of the river, and you are going to be there someday too."

Edgar was now smiling more broadly than he had smiled at any other time today. He replied, "It's a mountain! I'll be on the mountain waving to you down by the river." Edgar waved one of his hands. He then asked, "And are you going outside to see me off?"

Constance shot back, "Of course I will go outside to see you off."

Edgar said, "Oh, I see now. People usually are alive and walk around, then they die and get carried out. With you, they carry you in, you complain about dying, and then you walk out. Isn't that right?"

Constance replied, "Agnes and Martha just have to help me a little bit."

Edgar said, I suppose that were I to stay much longer, I would end up dancing with you, would I not?" With that, Edgar gave Constance a very soft embrace. He asked her, "Do you know that, other than you, there is no one alive today—at least not that I know of—who remembers my father?"

Constance replied, "That is surely a long time ago, but it still gives me sorrow." Neither Constance nor Edgar said any more to one another.

As Edgar turned away from Constance, he and Roadie both waved their hands briefly. They said, "Good-bye. Good-bye, everyone," and then they turned to the door.

Roadie was the first out the door, followed by William and then Edgar. Then Constance, helped by Martha and Agnes, came out slowly. Finally, Andrus, John, and all the children went outside to gather around Edgar's carriage before he left. In just a few moments, Edgar and Roadie were on their way down the road.

Wrap-Up

An exciting day that was! For the very first Christmas at what would become the Borthwick Parish Church, the people gathered there had experienced an amazing few hours. Edgar had shared his reminiscences and had told a wide variety of stories about his family, his spiritual experiences, the wars he had seen, the First Crusade, and politics. He had taught the Bible from his reading, also using his observations and knowledge of wildlife. He had given a message wherein he attempted to explain the concept of freedom, or at least to criticize feudalism, to people for whom freedom was still a far-off, almost unheard-of concept.

Looking over Edgar's life, I believe that he could have believed and spoken everything that he said in the foregoing story. Looking over the history of Scotland, I see that 1125 was the start of a long period of relative peace. The Scottish people historically have shown a strong determination to remain free from being dominated by England or by any other foreign power. Why couldn't Edgar have been one of the men who contributed to the idea of freedom for this world and advanced the cause of Christ?

Epilogue

The Families

In researching this book, I encountered more exciting stories about our families.

The Drummonds

The legend is that George, the illegitimate son of Andrew I of Hungary, accompanied the Aethelings into exile in Scotland. George's son Maurice is the ancestor of the clan.[1] The name Drummond apparently comes from the Scottish/Gaelic word *dromainn,* which can variously mean "back of the mountain," "ridge," and "high ground."

The Drummonds have been prominent in Scottish royalty and politics almost continuously since they settled in Scotland in the eleventh century. Most noteworthy is that in 1357, Annabella Drummond married John Stewart, who would later become the king of Scotland as Robert III. Also, Margaret Drummond married King of Scotland David II in 1364. In the twentieth century, James Eric Drummond (1876–1951) served as the first secretary-general of the League of Nations.[2]

The Leslies

There are several versions of the story of the Leslies. One is that a Hungarian nobleman named Walter de Leslin came from the castle of Leslyn in Hungary. The family in Scotland was thus started by

Walter's son, Barthlomew.[3] However, another version states that the Hungarian nobleman was named Baltorf.[4] Here I see vast potential for confusion, as the names Baltorf, Bartholomew, and even Borthwick are so similar that they may be naming one, two, or three different men, or a combination of men and their son(s).

Sources agree that Barthlomew was Margaret's "chamberlain." This cute story is told: As Margaret and Barthlomew were traveling in Scotland, they encountered a river swollen by heavy rain. They and the group they were with attempted to cross the river on horseback, but the force of the current was enough to throw Margaret from her horse. She was in danger of being drowned when Barthlomew, plunged into the stream to save her. He found that the best way to secure her was to grasp hold of her girdle. As Barthlomew struggled against the current to bring Margaret toward the riverbank, Margaret frequently exclaimed, "Grip fast." After this, she desired that this should be Barthlomew's motto. Thus, the phrase *Grip Fast* is prominent in the Leslie family crest.[5]

Barthlomew eventually married Beatrix, the sister of King Malcolm Canmore. Malcolm appointed Barthlomew to be the governor of Edinburgh Castle. Malcolm also granted to him an area of land that was then named Leslie (it had originally been named Lesslyn). According to this version of the story, the land's name is the origin of the name Leslie. Barthlomew was given the titles "Lord Leslie" and "Earl of Ross," thus the name of the family, Leslie.[6]

The Livingstones

The history agrees that there was a man named Livingus.[7] He likely came from Hungary. Another source theorizes that this man was a Saxon who met the Aethelings in England and who continued to Scotland with them in 1067.[8] In Scotland, the name Livingus was first known as Levingeston and eventually became Livingstone. One of the descendants of this family is David Livingstone, the famous African explorer of the late nineteenth century.

The Sinclairs

A man named Walderness Compte de Saint Clare of Normandy[9] is named as the ancestor of the Sinclair family. The name St. Clair may have been taken from the town of Saint-Clair-sur-Epte, between Paris and Rouen, although several other places with similar names have been mentioned. In Scotland, the name eventually changed to Sinclair, although some of this family have retained "St. Clair."

There are a number of legends, even contradictory stories, about the son of Walderness, William "the Seemly" St. Clair. He has become a legendary figure, as he accompanied Margaret from Hungary, but this is because Margaret later became famous as the queen of Scotland. At the time, Margaret, eleven or twelve years of age, was simply a daughter of Edward's. Edward, and then Edward's son Edgar, would have been St. Clair's primary concern.

The legend is that when the Battle of Hastings occurred in 1066, several of the St. Clair brothers fought with William the Conqueror, even after their family had previously fought against him in Normandy. William the Seemly, however, may have fought for either the Normans or the English, or he may not have participated at all at Hastings. After the Normans were victorious, it seems certain that William the Seemly accompanied Margaret and the Aethelings to Scotland in 1067, or at least met them again in Scotland, thus confirming that part of the legend. Margaret had even named him as her cupbearer.[10]

William was just settling in Scotland, probably near Rosslyn, when he died fighting against the Normans in about 1070. His son Henry then inherited his father's land. Later, during the reign of Alexander I in Scotland (1108–24), a son of William the Seemly named William de Sancto Claro was granted additional land at Rosslyn.

The Sinclairs seemed to develop a particular interest in religious artifacts and treasures. The Black Cross that Margaret possessed seemed to hold a considerable influence on the Sinclairs, even as centuries passed. Perhaps Scotland's possession of the cross even influenced the St. Clairs to travel to Scotland to remain close to the artifact. Later, the English took the Holyrood from the Scots, returned it, then retook it after various battles. It may have been destroyed, as the Protestant

Reformation in the 1600s turned to condemn any objects or symbols. However, another source states that it was saved and is now at the Holy Cross Abbey in Thurles, County Tipperary, Ireland.[11]

When the Knights Templar were ejected from Europe in 1307, some of them sought refuge in Scotland. As the Knights Templar apparently did take some religious objects or treasures with them to Scotland, the Sinclairs moved quickly to give the knights shelter. Today, the Masons, or Freemasons, maintain the legend that their organization began with the Knights Templar and the Sinclairs.[12] Also, there is evidence that some of the Sinclairs and Knights Templar took various items of treasure to America and placed these in remote hiding places. The assertion is that in 1398, Henry Sinclair traveled with several hundred men on a fleet of at least a dozen ships to explore Labrador, Nova Scotia, and Massachusetts.[13]

Beginning in 1446, the Sinclairs built the Rosslyn Chapel, which has now gained considerable worldwide fame following the book and the film *The Da Vinci Code.* The chapel is covered inside and out with intricate carvings in stone that symbolize Christianity, but it also shows many other objects and characters. Remarkably, some of the carvings show some types of flowers and maize (corn) that grow in the Americas, but these should have been unknown in Europe at the time, as the construction of the chapel was completed before Christopher Columbus sailed to North America. In the chapel, there is a carving of a knight on horseback; a woman holding a cross is seated next to him. This has been interpreted as William the Seemly and Margaret traveling to Scotland.[14]

The Borthwicks

As is noted in the preface, a man named Andreas came from Hungary with the Aethelings. He is thought to be the ancestor of the Borthwicks. Also, we know that the son-in-law of Grand Prince Yaroslav and Queen Ingigerd was Andras, who was helped by Edward the Exile to became Andrew I of Hungary. Considering the similarity of the names Andras, Andrew I, and Andreas, could there be a connection to the royal family line? In this case, no, as the descendants of Andrew I and Anastasia are well-known and do not include anyone named Andreas. After Anastasia, the remaining descendants of Yaroslav and Ingigerd are mostly known and do not include an Andreas. However, the extended family of Yaroslav is rather large, and there are some unknowns to be found. Possibly a DNA test might show some connection to the Borthwicks if descendants of Yaroslav can be found.

Another idea is that the Borthwicks came to Scotland with the Roman legions of Julius Caesar.[15] This assertion seems to me to border on fantasy. *Monarchs of Scotland* names Scotland's first king as Kenneth MacAlpine, starting in 841, the Romans arrived more than seven hundred years before that! In the Middle Ages, the Borthwicks did develop a reputation as fierce battlers; maybe this gave rise to the thought that "they must have been Romans."

The name Borthwick is supposed to be derived from "the Borthwick Water which lies between Selkirk and Roxburgh in the Scottish Borders,"[16] apparently a stream in the area. Is the spoken name supposed to mimic the sound of the water as it tumbles over rocks? Slightly more plausible to me is that the man Baltorf, whom I introduced in the discussion of the Leslies, may actually be the man who provided the beginning of the name Borthwick, as the two names have some similarity. A huge obstacle is that the name Borthwick was not used until sometime in the 1200s. It also went through several spelling variations. Trying to trace the connection to Andreas, or to Baltorf, is apparently impossible.

Andreas and William Sinclair certainly had a long friendship, starting with their trip from Hungry. In Scotland, the lands where they settled are the locations of the Borthwick Castle and the Rosslyn Chapel of the Sinclairs, which lands, south of Edinburgh, are not far from each other. Thus, the two families formed a strong friendship and alliance that continued for centuries beyond the 1070s. For example, in 1330 William Borthwick and William Sinclair were in Spain fighting a crusade together.[17] Then, in the 1440s, when (another)William Sinclair began construction of the Rosslyn Chapel, he employed (another) William Borthwick to serve as his cupbearer, a position of great honor. This William Borthwick is the same man who constructed the

Borthwick Castle in 1430 and was named the 1st Lord Borthwick in about 1452.[18]

Today, the Borthwick Castle stands at the end of a lengthy driveway. The Borthwick Parish Church and the Borthwick Parish School are just off the road at the beginning of the drive to the castle.

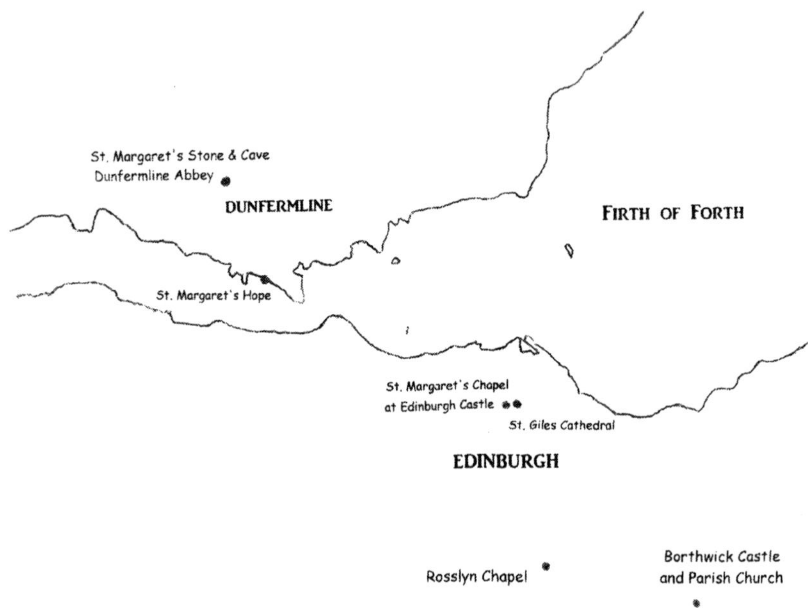

Edinburgh and Dunfermline

The Borthwick Castle Tower (*photo by author's family, August 2009*)

The Borthwick Castle and the Borthwick Parish Church
(*photo by author's family, August 2009*)

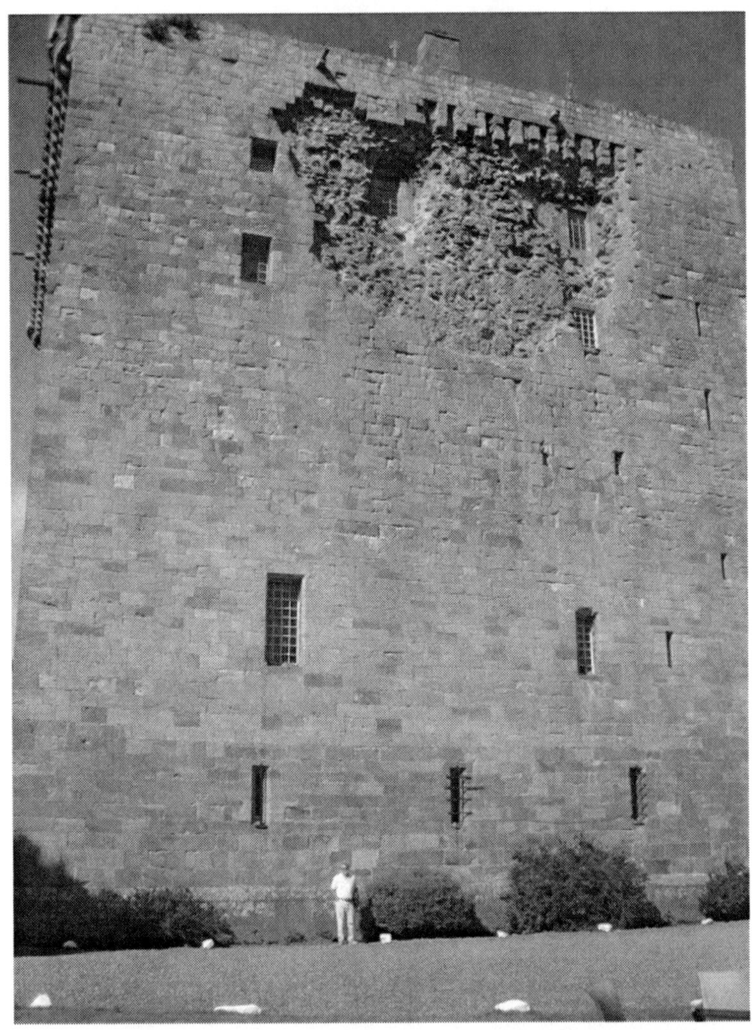

The author stands in front of the rear wall of the Borthwick Castle. This wall was damaged by 3 cannonballs fired in the year 1650 when the army of Oliver Cromwell invaded Scotland. When Cromwell demanded surrender, the inhabitants fled, thus sparing the castle from any further damage. (*photo by author's family, August 2009*)

Endnotes

1 Clifford Stanley Sims, "Leslie," in *The Origin and Significance of Scottish Surnames* (New York: Avenal Books, 1964), 67.

2 "Clan Drummond," *Wikipedia,* accessed August 12, 2015, http://en.wikipedia.org/wiki/Clan_Drummond

3 Sims, *Scottish surnames*, Leslie, page 67

4 Ibid.

5 Ibid.

6 Ibid.

7 Sims, *Scottish Surnames*, Livingstone, page 69

8 "Clan Livingstone," *ElectricScotland.com,* accessed August 12, 2015, http://www.electricscotland.com/webclans/htol/livings2.html

9 Niven Sinclair, William "the Seemly" Sinclair, First Baron of Roslin, accessed August 12, 2015 http://sinclair.quarterman.org/who/seemly.html

10 Sims, "Sinclair," in *Scottish Surnames,* 92.

11 "Holy Cross Abbey," Failte, Ireland, accessed August 12, 2015, http://www.discoverireland.ie/Arts-Culture-Heritage/holy-cross-abbey/63099

12 "Rosslyn Chapel, Templars and Masons," *Temple of Mysteries,* accessed March 2, 2015, http://www.templeofmysteries.com/rosslyn-chapel/rosslyn-chapel,-templars-&-masons/

13 Rick and Marty Lagina, "The Trail of the Templars," *The Curse of Oak Island, History.com,* accessed March 2, 2015, http://www.history.com/shows/the-curse-of-oak-island/videos/the-trail-of-the-templars?m=5189717d404fa&s=All&f=1&free=false. Episodes of the television show *The Curse of Oak Island* show the search for items of treasure that the producers believe that the Knights Templar brought to North America. See also "Sinclairs in Scotland," *History of Clan Sinclair,* accessed August 12, 2015, http://sinclair.quarterman.org/history/med/scotland.html

14 "Rosslyn Chapel and Roslin Castle," *Mysterious Britain,* accessed March 2, 2015, http://www.mysteriousbritain.co.uk/scotland/mid-lothian/featured-sites/rosslyn-chapel-roslin-castle.html (see image 2)

15 "Clan/Family Histories – Borthwick," *RampantScotland.com,* accessed August 12, 2015, http://www.rampantscotland.com/clans/blclanborthwick.htm

16 Lang Syne, "Borthwick," in LLC Books, ed., *History of Scotland by Period: Early Modern Scotland, Medieval Scotland, Prehistoric Scotland, Dál Riata, Edgar the Ætheling* (Memphis: General Books, 2010), 13.

17 Ibid., 15.

18 Ibid., 16–18.

Notes

The reader should note that Internet addresses, and even the content of an article, can change.

I cited an Internet site when appropriate after the introduction of a person, place, or object. I did not include a subsequent citation of an Internet site unless I took a direct quotation from that site.

In addition, I cite more than one Internet site when I provide information about a person, a place, or an object only when I found the specific information on an additional site.

All Scripture quotations are taken from the King James Version of the Bible.

About the Author

Alan Reed lives in Franklin, Tennessee with his wife Barbara. Our grown children are a son; Eric, and a daughter; Kirsten.

Kirsten Reed graduated in 2013 with a degree in Architecture from the University of Tennessee, and is working as a professional architect.

CPSIA information can be obtained at www.ICGtesting.com
Printed in the USA
LVOW07s1229091215

465802LV00003B/7/P

9 781512 718973